# LIFE IN CHRIST

## Register This New Book

### Benefits of Registering*

- ✓ FREE **replacements** of lost or damaged books
- ✓ FREE **audiobook** – *Pilgrim's Progress*, audiobook edition
- ✓ FREE information about new titles and other **freebies**

www.anekopress.com/new-book-registration

*See our website for requirements and limitations.

# Life in Christ

Lessons from Our Lord's
Miracles and Parables

The Miracles of Our Lord
Volume 3

## Charles H. Spurgeon

We love hearing from our readers. Please contact us
at www.anekopress.com/questions-comments with
any questions, comments, or suggestions.

*Life in Christ, Vol. 3*
© 2020 by Charles H. Spurgeon
All rights reserved.
Revised edition 2020

No part of this book may be reproduced, stored in a retrieval system, or transmitted in any form or by any means – electronic, mechanical, photocopying, recording, or otherwise, without written permission from the publisher.

Unless otherwise indicated, scripture quotations are taken from the New American Standard Bible® (NASB), copyright © 1960, 1962, 1963, 1968, 1971, 1972, 1973, 1975, 1977, 1995 by The Lockman Foundation. Used by permission. www.Lockman.org.

Scripture quotations marked (KJV) are from The Authorized (King James) Version. Rights in the Authorized Version in the United Kingdom are vested in the Crown. Reproduced by permission of the Crown's patentee, Cambridge University Press.

*Cover Design: Natalia Hawthorne*
*Cover Painting: Matt Philleo*
*Editor: Paul Miller*
Printed in the United States of America

Aneko Press
www.anekopress.com
Aneko Press, Life Sentence Publishing, and our logos are trademarks of
Life Sentence Publishing, Inc.
203 E. Birch Street
P.O. Box 652
Abbotsford, WI 54405

**RELIGION / Christian Life / Spiritual Growth**
Paperback ISBN: 978-1-62245-692-5
eBook ISBN: 978-1-62245-693-2
10  9  8  7  6  5  4  3  2  1

Available where books are sold

# Contents

**Ch. 1:** Beloved, yet Afflicted ................................................................. 1

**Ch. 2:** A Mystery! Saints Sorrowing and Jesus Glad! ........................ 7

**Ch. 3:** Even Now ..................................................................................... 25

**Ch. 4:** Though He Were Dead ............................................................. 43

**Ch. 5:** The Believer Catechized .......................................................... 59

**Ch. 6:** The Master ................................................................................. 77

**Ch. 7:** Jesus Wept .................................................................................. 95

**Ch. 8:** Might Have Been, or May Be ................................................ 113

**Ch. 9:** The Sphere of Instrumentality ............................................. 125

**Ch. 10:** Unbinding Lazarus ................................................................ 143

*Charles H. Spurgeon – A Brief Biography* ......................................... 161

*Other Similar Titles* ............................................................................... 165

## Chapter 1

# Beloved, yet Afflicted

*Lord, behold, he whom You love is sick.* (John 11:3)

That disciple whom Jesus loved is not at all reluctant to record that Jesus loved Lazarus too. There are no jealousies among those who are chosen by the Well-beloved. Jesus loved Mary, Martha, and Lazarus. It is a happy thing when an entire family lives in the love of Jesus. They were a favored trio, and yet, just as the serpent came into the garden of Eden, so sorrow entered their quiet household at Bethany.

Lazarus was sick. They all felt that if Jesus were there, disease would flee at His presence. What, then, should they do but let Him know of their trial? Lazarus was near death's door, and so his tender sisters at once reported the fact to Jesus, saying, *Lord, behold, he whom You love is sick*. Many times since then that same message has been sent to our Lord, for in very many cases He has chosen His people in the furnace of affliction. Of the Master it is said, *He Himself took our infirmities and carried away our diseases* (Matthew 8:17), and it is therefore not an extraordinary thing for the members of the body to be conformed to their Head in this matter.

**Notice, first, a fact mentioned in the text**
*Lord, behold, he whom You love is sick.* The sisters were somewhat astonished that it should be so, for the word "behold" implies a measure of

surprise. "We love him, and we would make him well now if we could. You love him, and yet he remains sick. You can heal him with one word. Why, then, is Your loved one sick?" Have you not, dear sick friend, often wondered how your painful or lingering disease could be consistent with your being chosen, called, and made one with Christ? I dare say this has greatly troubled you, and yet in very truth it is by no means strange, but is to be expected.

We do not need to be astonished that the man whom the Lord loves is sick, for he is only a man. The love of Jesus does not separate us from the common necessities and infirmities of human life. Men of God are still men. The covenant of grace is not a charter of exemption from fever, rheumatism, or asthma. The bodily ailments that come upon us because of our flesh will stay with us to the tomb, for Paul says, *While we are in this tent, we groan* (2 Corinthians 5:4).

Those whom the Lord loves are more likely to be sick since they are under a special discipline. It is written, *Those whom the Lord loves He disciplines, and He scourges every son whom He receives* (Hebrews 12:6). Affliction of some sort is one of the marks of the true born-again child of God, and it frequently happens that the trial takes the form of illness. Will we therefore wonder that we have to take our turn in the bed of sickness? If Job, David, and Hezekiah each had to endure pain, who are we that we would be amazed because we are in poor health?

It is not surprising that we are sick if we reflect upon the great benefit that often flows to us from it. I do not know what specific improvement might have been worked in Lazarus, but many disciples of Jesus would have been of little use if they had not been afflicted. Strong men are apt to be harsh, domineering, and unsympathetic, and therefore they need to be put into the furnace and melted down. I have known Christian women who never would have been so gentle, tender, wise, experienced, and holy if they had not been mellowed by physical pain. There are fruits in God's garden as well as in man's that never ripen until they are bruised. Young women who are apt to be volatile, conceited, or talkative are often trained to be full of sweetness and light by sickness after sickness, by which they are taught to sit at Jesus' feet. Many have been able to say with the psalmist, *It is good for me that I was afflicted, that I may learn Your statutes* (Psalm 119:71). For this reason, even those who are highly favored and blessed among women (Luke 1:28) might feel a sword piercing through their hearts at times.

This sickness of the Lord's loved ones is often for the good of others. Lazarus was permitted to be sick and die so that by his death and resurrection the apostles could be benefited. His sickness was *for the glory of God* (John 11:4). Throughout these two thousand years that have succeeded Lazarus' sickness, all believers have been getting good out of it, and we are still being helped today because he suffered and died.

The church and the world can obtain much advantage through the sorrows of good people. The careless may be awakened, the doubting may be convinced, the ungodly may be converted, and the mourner may be comforted through our testimony in sickness. If this is so, why would we want to avoid pain and weakness? Are we not quite willing that our friends would say of us also, *Lord, behold, he whom You love is sick*?

**Our text, however, not only records a fact, but mentions a report of that fact:**
*The sisters sent word to Him* (John 11:3). Let us keep up constant communication with our Lord about everything.

> Sing a hymn to Jesus when thy heart is faint;
> Tell it all to Jesus, comfort or complaint.

Jesus knows all about us, but it can provide much consolation for us to pour out our hearts before Him. When John the Baptist's brokenhearted disciples saw their leader beheaded, they *took away the body and buried it; and they went and reported to Jesus* (Matthew 14:12). They could not have done better. When you have any trouble, send a message to Jesus; do not keep your misery to yourself.

There is a pleasant hope about telling Jesus, for He is sure to support His friends in it. You can go to Jesus and ask, *Most gracious Lord, why am I sick? I thought I was useful while in health, and now I can do nothing; why is this?* He may show you why, or if not, He will make you willing to bear His will with patience without knowing why. He can bring His truth to your mind to cheer you, He can strengthen your heart by His presence, He can send you unexpected comfort, and He can cause you to glory in your afflictions. *Trust in Him at all times, O people; pour out your heart before Him; God is a refuge for us* (Psalm 62:8). Mary and Martha did not send to tell Jesus in vain, and no one seeks His face in vain.

Remember, too, that Jesus may give healing. It would not be wise to claim to live by faith and reject the physician and his medicine any more than it would be wise to avoid the butcher and the tailor and expect to be fed and clothed by faith. However, this would be far better than forgetting the Lord completely and trusting in human help only.

Healing for both body and soul must be sought from God. We make use of medicines, but these can do nothing apart from the Lord, *who heals all your diseases* (Psalm 103:3). We can tell Jesus about our aches and pains, our gradual decline, and our hacking coughs. Some people are afraid to go to God about their health. They pray for the forgiveness of sin, but they are afraid to ask the Lord to remove a headache; yet certainly if the hairs on the outside of our head are all numbered by God, it is not much more of a condescension for Him to relieve throbs and pressures inside the head. Our big things must be very little to the great God, and our little things cannot be much less.

It is a proof of the greatness of the mind of God that while ruling the heavens and the earth, He is not so consumed by these great concerns as to be forgetful of the least pain or need of any one of His poor children. We can go to Him about our failing breath, for He first gave us lungs and life. We can tell Him about the eye that grows dim and the ear that loses hearing, for He made them both. We can mention the swollen knee, the arthritic finger, the stiff neck, and the sprained foot, for He made all these, redeemed them all, and will raise them all from the grave. Go at once, and say, *Lord, behold, he whom You love is sick.*

## Thirdly, let us notice in the case of Lazarus a result that we might not have expected.

Undoubtedly when Mary and Martha sent word to Jesus, they hoped to see Lazarus recover as soon as the messenger reached the Master; but they were not gratified in this way. For two days the Lord remained in the same place, and not until He knew that Lazarus was dead did He talk about going to Judea.

This teaches us that Jesus can be informed of our trouble, and yet might act as if He were indifferent to it. We must not expect that prayer for recovery will be answered in every case, for if so, nobody would die who had family, friend, or acquaintance to pray for him. In our prayers for the lives of beloved children of God, we must not forget that there is one prayer that may be contradicting ours, for Jesus prays, *Father, I desire that they also, whom You have given Me, be with Me where I am, so that they may see My glory which You have given Me* (John 17:24). We pray that they may remain with us, but when we recognize that Jesus wants them above, what can we do but admit His greater claim and say, *Not as I will, but as You will* (Matthew 26:39)?

In our own case, we can ask the Lord to raise us up, and although He loves us, He might allow us to grow worse and worse, and at last die. Hezekiah had fifteen years added to his life, but we might not have the reprieve of a single day. Never set such importance on the life of any one dear to you, or even on your own life, as to be rebellious against the Lord. If you hold the life of any dear one with too tight a hand, you are making a rod for your own back. If you love your own earthly life too well, you are making a thorny pillow for your dying bed. We often idolize children, or other individuals or leaders we look up to. We might as well make a god of clay and worship it, as the Hindus are said to do, as worship our fellow humans, for what are they but clay? Will dust be so dear to us that we quarrel with our God about it? If our Lord allows us to suffer, let us not complain. He must do that for us which is kindest and best, for He loves us better than we love ourselves.

Did I hear you say, "Yes, Jesus allowed Lazarus to die, but He raised him up again"? I answer that He is the resurrection and the life to us also (John 11:25). Be comforted concerning the departed. *Your brother will rise again* (John 11:23), and all of us whose hope is in Jesus will partake in our Lord's resurrection. Not only will our souls live, but our bodies, too, will be raised incorruptible (1 Corinthians 15:52). The grave will serve as a refining pot (Proverbs 17:3), and this vile body will emerge vile no more.

Some Christians are greatly encouraged by the thought of living until the Lord comes, and so escaping death. I confess that I think this is no great gain, for so far from having any benefit over those who have died, those who are alive and remain at His coming will miss one point of fellowship – in not dying and rising like their Lord. Beloved, all things are yours, and death is specifically mentioned in the list; therefore do not dread it, but rather "long for evening to undress, that you may rest with God."

**I will close with a question**
*Jesus loved Martha and her sister and Lazarus* (John 11:5). Does Jesus love you in a special way? Sadly, many sick people have no evidence of any special love of Jesus toward them, for they have never sought His face or trusted in Him. Jesus might say to them, *I never knew you* (Matthew 7:23), for they have turned their backs upon His blood and His cross. Answer, dear friend, this question to your own heart: Do you love Jesus? If so, you love Him because He first loved you (1 John 4:19). Are you trusting Him? If so, that faith of yours is the proof that He has loved you from before the foundation of the world, for faith is the sign by which He pledges His faithfulness to His beloved.

If Jesus loves you, and you are sick, let all the world see how you glorify God in your sickness. Let friends and nurses see how the beloved of the Lord are cheered and comforted by Him. Let your holy submission astonish them and cause them to admire your Beloved, who is so gracious to you that He makes you happy in pain and joyful at the gates of the grave. If your Christian religion is worth anything, it should support you now, and it will compel unbelievers to see that he whom the Lord loves is better off when he is sick than the ungodly are when they are full of health and vigor.

If you do not know that Jesus loves you, you lack the brightest star that can cheer the night of sickness. It would indeed be a terrible calamity to hope that you will not die as you now are, and to pass into another world without enjoying the love of Jesus. Seek His face at once, and it might be that your current sickness is a part of the way of love by which Jesus will bring you to Himself. *Lord, heal all these sick ones in soul and in body. Amen.*

## Chapter 2

# A Mystery! Saints Sorrowing and Jesus Glad!

*Jesus then said to them plainly, "Lazarus is dead, and I am glad for your sakes that I was not there, so that you may believe; but let us go to him."* (John 11:14-15)

There lived in the little village of Bethany a very happy family. There was neither father nor mother in it, but the household consisted of the unmarried brother Eleazar, or Lazarus, and his sisters, Martha and Mary. They lived together in unity so good and pleasant that the Lord commanded the blessing there of life for evermore. This affectionate trio all loved the Lord Jesus Christ, and they were frequently favored with His company. They kept an open house whenever the great preacher came that way. Both for the Master and the disciples, there was always a table, a bed, and a candlestick in the prophet's chamber (2 Kings 4:10), and sometimes magnificent feasts were prepared for the whole company. They were very happy, and they rejoiced much to think that they could be helpful in regard to the necessities of one so poor, and yet so honored, as the Lord Jesus.

But sadly, affliction shows up everywhere. Virtue may guard the door, but difficulty and sorrow are not to be excluded from the homestead. *Man is born for trouble, as sparks fly upward* (Job 5:7). Even if the fuel is a log of sweet-smelling sandalwood, the sparks must still rise, and even so the best of families must experience affliction. Lazarus became sick. It was a fatal sickness beyond the power of physicians. The first thought of the sisters was to send for their friend Jesus. They knew that one word from His lips would restore their brother. There was no absolute need for Him to risk His safety by traveling to Bethany, they thought, for He only had to speak the word, and their brother would be made whole.

With glowing hopes and moderated concern, they sent a tender message to Jesus: *Lord, behold, he whom You love is sick* (John 11:3). Jesus heard it, and sent back the answer that had much comfort in it, but could hardly compensate for His own absence: *This sickness is not to end in death, but for the glory of God, so that the Son of God may be glorified by it* (John 11:4).

Poor Lazarus did not recover after the message came. He was a little more cheerful because he heard that his sickness was not unto death, but his pain did not lessen. The cold sweat of death gathered on his brow. His tongue was dry. He was full of pain and afflicted with anguish. At last he passed through the iron gate of death, and his corpse rested there before the eyes of the weeping sisters.

Why was Jesus not there? Why did He not come? As tenderhearted as He always was, what could have made Him unkind now? Why had He waited? Why was He so long in coming? How could His words be true? He said, *This sickness is not to end in death*, and there lies the good man cold in death, and the mourners are gathering for the funeral. Look at Martha! She had been sitting up every night watching her poor brother. No care could have been more constant, no tenderness more excessive. There was no remedy available to her that she did not try. She gathered this herb and the other, and she gave Lazarus all sorts of medicinal drinks and nourishing foods. She anxiously watched until her eyes were red for lack of sleep.

Jesus could have spared her all this. Why didn't He? He only had to wish it, and the flush of health would have returned to the cheeks of Lazarus. There would have been no more need of this weary care and this killing watchfulness. What was Jesus doing? Martha was willing to serve Him, but would He not serve her? She has even troubled herself about much serving for His sake (Luke 10:41), giving Him not only necessities, but delicacies, and will He not give her what is so desirable to her heart, so essential to her happiness – her brother's life? How can He send her a promise that He does not seem to keep? How can He tease her with hope and cast down her faith?

As for Mary, she has been sitting still at her brother's side, listening to his dying words, repeating in his ear the gracious words of Jesus that she had heard as she sat at His feet. She was catching the last words of her dying brother, thinking less about the medicine and the diet than Martha did, but thinking more about his spiritual health and about his soul's enjoyment. She has tried to lift up the sinking spirits of her beloved brother with words like these: "He will come. He may wait, but I know Him. His heart is very kind, and He will be here. Even if He lets you sleep in death, it will only be for a little while. He raised the widow's son at the gates of Nain (Luke 7:15), and He will certainly raise you, whom He loves far more. Have you not heard how He wakened the daughter of Jairus (Mark 5:42)? Brother, He will come and awaken you, and we will have many happy hours yet. We will have this as a special token of love from our Master and our Lord – that He raised you from the dead."

But why, why was she not spared those bitter tears that ran scalding down her cheeks when she saw that her brother was really dead? She could not believe it. She kissed his forehead, and oh, how cold was that marble brow! She lifted up his hand and said, "He cannot be dead, for Jesus said this sickness was not unto death." However, the hand fell nerveless by her side. Her brother was really a corpse, and decay soon set in. Then she knew that the beloved clay was not exempt from all the dishonor that decay brings to the human body.

Poor Mary! Jesus loved you, it is said, but this is a strange way of showing His love. Where is He? He lingers miles away. He knows that your brother is sick. Yes, He knows that he is dead, and yet He still remains where He is. Oh, what a sorrowful mystery that the compassion of such a tender Savior would sink so far below their plumb line to gauge, or that His mercy would range so high beyond their power to reach.

Jesus is now talking about the death of His friend. Let us listen to His words. Maybe we can find the key to His actions in the words of His lips. How surprising! He does not say, "I regret that I have waited so long." He does not say, "I should have hurried, but even now it is not too late." No! Hear and marvel! Wonder of wonders! He says, *I am glad . . . that I was not there.* He says that He was *glad*! Is not the word out of place? By this time, Lazarus stinks in his tomb, and here the Savior is glad! Martha and Mary are weeping their eyes out for sorrow, and yet their friend, Jesus, is glad! It is strange; it is beyond strange!

However, we can rest assured that Jesus knows better than we do, and our faith can therefore sit still and try to figure out His meaning when our reason cannot find it at first. *I am glad*, He said, *for your sakes that I was not there, so that you may believe.* Ah! We see it now. Christ is not glad because of sorrow, but only on account of the result of the sorrow. He knew that this temporary trial would help His disciples to a greater faith, and He so values their growth in faith that He is even glad of the sorrow that causes it. It is as if He said, "I am glad for your sakes that I was not there to prevent the trouble, for now that it is come, it will teach you to believe in Me. This will be much better for you than to have been spared the affliction."

We plainly have the principle here that our Lord, in His infinite wisdom and superabundant love, sets so high a value upon His people's faith that He will not keep them from those trials by which faith is strengthened. Let us try to press the wine of consolation from the cluster of the text. In three cups we will preserve the pleasant juice as it flows forth from the winepress of meditation. Jesus Christ was glad that the trial had come:

1. For the strengthening of the faith of the apostles.

2. For strengthening the faith of the family.

3. For giving faith to others.

In the forty-fifth verse of John 11, we see that *many of the Jews who came to Mary, and saw what He had done, believed in Him.*

## Jesus Christ designed the death and resurrection of Lazarus for the strengthening of the faith of the apostles.

This was done in two ways. Not only would the trial itself tend to strengthen their faith, but the remarkable deliverance that Christ gave to them out of it would certainly minister to the growth of their confidence in Him.

1. Let us observe that the trial itself would certainly tend to increase the apostle's faith. Faith that is not tested can still be true faith, but it is sure to be little faith. I believe in the existence of faith in people who have no trials, but that is as far as I can go. I am persuaded, brethren, that where there is no trial, faith just draws breath enough to live, but that is all. Faith, like the fabled salamander, has fire for its native element. Faith never prospers as well as when all things are against it. Storms train the faith, and the lightnings illuminate it. When a calm reigns on the sea, you can spread the sails however you want, but the ship will not move to its harbor. When the ocean is at rest, the ship sleeps, too.

However, once the winds come howling forth and the waters lift themselves up, then even though the vessel rocks, her deck is washed with waves, and her mast creaks under the pressure of the full and swelling sail; yet it is then that she makes headway toward her desired haven. No flowers wear so lovely a blue as those that grow at the foot of the frozen glacier. No stars are as bright as those that glisten in the polar sky. No water is as sweet as that which springs amid the desert sand. No faith is as precious as that which lives and triumphs in adversity.

This is why the Lord says, by the mouth of the prophet, *I will also leave in the midst of thee an afflicted and poor people, and they shall trust in the name of the* LORD (Zephaniah 3:12 KJV). Why the afflicted and poor? Because there is a certain willingness in the afflicted and poor among the Lord's people to trust in the Lord. God does not say, "I will leave in the midst of you a prosperous and rich people, and they will trust." No! The prosperous and rich hardly seem to have such capacity for faith as the afflicted ones have. Rather, God says, I will leave in the midst of you an afflicted and poor people, and they, by reason of their very affliction and poverty, will be the more graciously disposed to place their faith in the Lord.

Untried faith is always small in stature, and it is likely to remain small as long as it is without trials. There is no room in the gentle pools of ease for faith to gain leviathan proportions. Faith must dwell in the stormy sea in order to become one of the main ways of God. Tried faith brings experience, and every one of you who are men and women of experience know that experience makes Christianity become more real to you. You cannot know the bitterness of sin or the sweetness of forgiveness until you have felt both. You do not know your own weakness until you have been compelled to go through the rivers, and you would never have known God's strength if you had not been supported amid the floods.

All the talk about Christianity that is not based upon experience is mere talk. If we have little experience, we cannot speak as convincingly and with as much certainty as they can whose experience has been more deep and profound. Once when I was preaching about the faithfulness of God in times of trial in the earlier days of my ministry, my venerable grandfather was sitting in the pulpit behind me. He suddenly stood up and took my place in front of the pulpit. He said, "My grandson can preach this as a matter of theory, but I can tell it to you as a matter of experience, for I have done business upon the great waters, and I have seen the works of the Lord for myself." There is an accumulation of force in the testimony of one who has personally experienced that which others can only speak of as though they had seen it in a map or in a picture.

Travelers who write from their easy chairs what they have seen from their studies may write books to consume the idle hours of those who stay at home, but he who is about to travel to regions full of danger seeks a guide who has really walked the road. The casual writer may excel in ornate words, but the actual traveler has real and valuable wisdom.

Faith increases in strength, assurance, and intensity the more it is exercised with affliction and the more it has been cast down and lifted up again. Do not let this, though, discourage those who are young in faith. You will have enough trials without seeking for them. The full portion will be measured out to you in due season. Meanwhile, if you cannot yet claim the result of long experience, thank God for what grace you have. Praise Him for that which you have attained. Walk according to that capacity, and you will have more and more of the blessing of God until your faith removes mountains and conquers impossibilities.

It might be asked what the method is by which trial strengthens faith. We could answer in various ways. Trial takes away many of the impediments of faith. Carnal security is the worst enemy to confidence in God. If I sit down and say, *Soul, you have many goods laid up for many years to come; take your ease, eat, drink and be merry* (Luke 12:19), then faith's road is barricaded. However, adversity sets the barn on fire, and the *many goods laid up for many years to come* cease to block the path of faith.

Oh, blessed axe of sorrow that clears a pathway for me to my God by cutting down the thick trees of my earthly comforts! When I say, as in Psalm 30:6-7, "My mountain stands firm. *I will never be moved,*" the visible fortification rather than the invisible protector engages my attention; but when the great earthquake shakes the rocks and the mountain is swallowed up, I fly to the immovable Rock of Ages to build my confidence on high. Worldly ease is a great enemy to faith. It loosens the joints of holy valor and snaps the sinews of sacred courage. The balloon never rises until the cords are cut. Affliction does this sharp service for believing souls. While the wheat sleeps comfortably in the husk, it is useless to man. It must be threshed out of its resting-place before its value can be known. Trial grabs the arrow of faith from the resting-place of the quiver and shoots it against the foe.

Affliction is also of much service for faith when it exposes the weakness of the creature. This trial showed the apostles that they must not depend upon the goodness of any one person, for although Lazarus may have entertained them and filled their little bag with food, yet Lazarus died, and Mary will die, and Martha will die, and all friends must die; this would teach them not to look to broken cisterns, but to run to the ever-flowing fountain.

Oh, dear friends, we are in much danger of making idols of our mercies! God gives us His temporal blessings as refreshments by the way, and then immediately we forget God and trust our riches. It is of the Lord's mercy that these idols are broken in pieces. He withers the gourds under which we sat in comfortable shade (Jonah 4:7) so that we will lift up our cry to Him and trust in Him alone. The emptiness of the creature is a lesson we are slow to learn, and we must have it beaten into us by the rod of affliction; but this lesson must be learned, or else faith can never grow strong.

Furthermore, trial is of special service to faith when it drives faith to God. I make a sad confession, over which I mourn, that when my soul is happy and things prosper, I do not generally live as near to God as I do in the midst of shame and contempt and when my spirit is cast down. *O my God, how dear You are to my soul in the night. When the sun goes down, O bright and morning star, how sweetly You shine!*

When the world's bread is sugared and buttered, we devour it until we grow sick. However, when the world changes our diet, fills our mouth with vinegar, and makes our drink gall and wormwood, then we cry out for our dear God again. When the world's wells are full of sweet but poisonous water, we pitch our tents at the well's mouth and drink again and again, forgetting the well of Bethlehem that is within the gate. However, when earth's water becomes bitter like the stream of Marah, then we turn away all sick and weak, and we cry after the water of life, *Spring up, O well!* (Numbers 21:17). Afflictions bring us to our God in the same way as the barking dog drives the wandering sheep to the shepherd's hand.

Trial also has a hardening effect upon faith. Just as the Spartan lads were prepared for fighting by the sharp discipline of their boyish days, so God's servants are trained for war by the afflictions that He sends upon them in the early days of their spiritual lives. We must run with footmen, or we will never be able to contend with horses (Jeremiah 12:5). We must be thrown into the water, or we will never learn to swim. We must hear the whizzing of the bullets, or we will never become veteran soldiers. The gardener knows that if his flowers were always kept in a greenhouse, they would quickly die during a cold night if they were put outside suddenly. So he does not give them too much heat, but exposes them a little at a time and gets them used to the cold so that they can live in the open air. In the same way, the only wise God does not put His servants in greenhouses and rear them delicately, but He exposes them to trials and difficulty so that they will know how to bear them when they come.

If you want to ruin your son, never let him know a hardship. When he is a child, carry him in your arms; when he becomes a youth, keep pampering him; and when he becomes a man, continue to spoil him – and you will succeed in producing an absolute fool. If you want to prevent him from being made useful in the world, guard him from every kind of work. Do not allow him to struggle. Wipe the sweat from his dainty brow and say, "Dear child, you will never have another task so difficult." Pity him when he should be punished, give him all that he wants, prevent all disappointments, and turn away all troubles – and you will certainly train him to be a reprobate and to break your heart. However, put him where he must work, wisely expose him to difficulties – and in this way you will make him a man. When he comes to do man's work and to bear man's trial, he will be ready for either.

My Master does not daintily cradle His children when they ought to run alone. When they begin to run, He does not always put out His arm for them to lean upon, but He lets them tumble down and scrape their knees, because then they will learn to walk more carefully. They will learn to stand upright by the strength that faith confers upon them.

You can see, dear friends, that Jesus Christ was glad that His disciples were blessed by trouble. Will you think about this, you who are so troubled today? Jesus Christ does sympathize with you, but He does so wisely, and He says, *I am glad for your sakes that I was not there.* He is glad that your husband is taken away, that your child is buried. He is glad that your business does not prosper. He is glad that you have those aches and pains and that you have such a weak body. He is glad for this to the intent that you may believe. You would never have possessed the precious faith that now supports you if the trial of your faith had not been like unto fire. You are a tree that never would have rooted so well if the wind had not rocked you back and forth, causing you to take a firm hold upon the precious truths of the covenant of grace.

2. Let us notice, also, that the deliverance that Christ brought about by the resurrection of Lazarus was also intended to strengthen the faith of the apostles. Christ can work even in the most difficult circumstances. What a situation they were now in! This was a case that had come to the very worst. Lazarus was not merely dead, but he had been buried. The stone had been rolled to the mouth of the sepulcher. Even worse, his body had begun to decay. There are so many miracles here that I must describe the resurrection of Lazarus not as one miracle only, but as a mass of wonders.

We will not go into detail, but suffice it to say that we cannot suppose anything to be a more amazing demonstration of divine strength than the restoration of health and life to a body through which the worms did creep and crawl. Yet even in this very worst case, Christ is not perplexed. This was a case where human power evidently could do nothing. Bring the violin and the harp, and let music try its work. Physician, bring your most powerful medicine and see what you can do. What! Does your medicinal mixture fail? The physician turns away disgusted, for the stench will destroy the physician's life before he is able to restore the corpse. Now seek all around the world and ask those who are as powerful as Herod with his soldiers, or Caesar on the imperial throne: "Can you do anything here?" No, they cannot, for death sits with his terrible smile laughing at them all. He says, "I have Lazarus beyond your reach." Yet Jesus Christ wins the day.

Divine sympathy became most evident. Jesus wept when He thought about Lazarus and his weeping sisters (John 11:35). We do not find it often said that He wept. He was *a man of sorrows and acquainted with grief* (Isaiah 53:3), but those were precious and rare drops that He shed over that dead body. He could do no more when He thought about Jerusalem (Luke 19:41), and He did no less when He was thinking about Lazarus.

What an exhibition these disciples had of the divine power, as well as the divine sympathy! Christ simply says, *Lazarus, come forth* (John 11:43), and death could hold his captive no longer. Lazarus came forth from the grave, restored to perfect health.

Do you not think that all this would tend to confirm the apostles' faith? It seems to me to be a part of the best education they could possibly receive for their future ministry. I think I see the apostles later locked up in prison. They are condemned to die, but Peter comforts John by saying, "He can bring us out of prison. Do you not remember how He brought Lazarus out of his grave? He can certainly appear for us and set us free." When they went forth to preach to sinners, how they would be strengthened by remembering these experiences! Their hearers were corrupt, depraved, and immoral. The apostles went into the midst of the worst conditions of human nature, and yet they did not fear for the result, for they knew that decaying Lazarus had been revived at Christ's word. Peter would argue, "Did not Christ restore Lazarus when his body was stinking and decayed? He can certainly bring the most reprobate hearts to the obedience of the truth. He can certainly raise the vilest of the vile to new life."

Many of the apostolic churches had strayed. They had unworthy members in them, but this would not assail the faith of the apostles too much, for they would say, "That same Christ who raised up Lazarus can still make Sardis, Pergamos, and Thyatira to be a praise in the earth. Churches that seem to be corrupt and foul in the nostrils of the Most High can still be made a brightness and glory and a sweet-selling savor unto Him." I am persuaded that very often such a miracle as this would recur to them and strengthen them in the times of their suffering and labor, and would make them able to bear afflictions, and even martyrdom itself, in confidence in Christ.

I will not say more about this because this seems obvious enough. Do not, though, forget the principle we are trying to bring out – that in the case of the apostles, Christ considered it worth any cost for them to have strong faith. No matter what pain it cost Mary and Martha, or in what grief it might involve Him or His apostles, they must bear it because the result was so exceedingly beneficial.

The surgeon handles the knife without tears; even though the cut is sharp, he knows it will cure. The mother puts the medicine to the child's mouth, and the child cries, and heaves, and loathes the bitterness, but the mother says, "Drink it all up, my child," because she knows there is life in every drop. In the same way, Christ is glad for the apostles' sake that He was not there, for the purpose that they would believe.

**Jesus Christ also cared about the good of the family.**
Mary and Martha had faith, but it was not very strong, for they suspected Christ's love when they said, *Lord, if You had been here, my brother would not have died* (John 11:21). There was a sort of half-murmur: "Why were You not here? Do You love us? Then why did You wait?" They certainly doubted His power. Although Martha could believe in the resurrection in general (John 11:24), she could not believe in the present resurrection for her brother. She said, *He has been dead four days* (John 11:39). She had faith, but it was very weak. Christ therefore sent the trial to Mary and Martha for their sakes, and He was glad to send it so that they might believe.

Observe, dear friends, that these were select favorites of the Lord Jesus Christ. He loves all His elect, but those three were as the darlings of the family, elect among the elect. They were three special favorites upon whom very distinguishing regard was set, and therefore it was that He sent them a special trial. The jeweler, if he takes up a stone and finds that it is not very precious, will not spend much care in cutting it; but when he gets a rare diamond of the finest quality, then he will be sure to cut, and cut, and cut again. When the Lord finds a saint whom He loves much, He may spare other people trials and troubles, but He certainly will not spare His well-beloved one. The more beloved you are, the more of the rod you will have.

It is a solemn thing to be a favorite of heaven. It is something to be sought after and to be rejoiced in, but to be part of the King's council chamber involves such work for faith that flesh and blood might draw back from the painful blessing. The gardener gets a tree, and if it is a common type, he will let it grow as it wills and will take what fruit comes from it naturally; but if it is a very rare kind, he likes to have every bough in its proper place so that it can bear well. He often takes out his knife and cuts here and there because, he says, "That is a favorite tree, and it is one that bears such fruit that I want much from it, and I do not want to leave anything at all that might cause it harm."

You who are God's favorites must not marvel at trials, but must instead keep your door wide open for them. When they come in, say, "Hail, messenger of the King! The sound of your Master's feet is behind you. You are welcome here, for your Master sent you" (2 Kings 6:32).

The special trial was attended with a special visit. Maybe Jesus would not have come to Bethany if Lazarus had not been dead; but as soon as there is a corpse in the house, Christ is in the house, too. O Christian, it will do much for your comfort and for the strengthening of your faith if Christ comes to you in your troubles. If you do not see any smiles in His face in your prosperity, you will not be without them in your adversity. The Lord Jesus will go out of His way to see you.

A mother can let her child run around and play, and she often hardly notices him when he is well; but when he cries, "My head, my head!" how tender she is toward him (2 Kings 4:19). How all the acts of love and the caresses of affection are lavished upon the little sick one! It will be the same with you, and in receiving these special visits, you will know that you are highly favored above the rest.

This special visit was attended with special fellowship. *Jesus wept* (John 11:35). He wept with those who wept. You will have Jesus sitting by the bedside and weeping with you when you are sick. You might be well and strong and have only a little fellowship with Christ now, but when you are sick, He will be there with you. Though you might walk along the green grass without the Savior, when you come into the midst of the fire, like Shadrach, Meshach, and Abed-nego, you will not be without Him then (Daniel 3:25).

There is no fellowship with Christ that is as near and sweet as that which comes to us when we are in deep trials. Then the Father opens His heart and takes His child, not upon His knee, but to His very heart, and tells him to lay his head upon His beating chest. Christ will reveal His secrets to you when the world is against you and trials surround you. *The secret of the* Lord *is for those who fear Him, and He will make them know His covenant* (Psalm 25:14), but they will never have such discoveries of that secret and that covenant as when they most need it – in the darkest and most trying times. It is then that there are special loves, special trials, special visits, and special fellowship.

You will soon have special deliverance. In days to come, you will talk about these trials. You will say, "I tormented myself and worried over it, but if I could have seen the end as well as the beginning, I would have said,

> 'Sweet affliction! Sweet affliction!
> Thus to bring my Savior near.'"

I tell you, you will yet sit under your own vine, and under your own fig tree (Micah 4:4), and talk to poor tried saints, and say, "Do not be cast down, for I cried unto the Lord and He heard me, *and delivered me from all my fears*" (Psalm 34:4). Maybe in heaven it will be part of your happiness to remember God's love to you in your tribulations.

> There on a green and flowery mount
>   Our weary souls shall sit,
> And with transporting joys recount
>   The labors of our feet.

Will we not tell angels, principalities, and powers about the faithfulness of Christ? We will tell all heaven that His *love is as strong as death, His jealousy is as severe as Sheol,* and that *many waters cannot quench love, nor will rivers overflow it* (Song of Solomon 8:6-7). What do you say, my friend, you who are under the disciplining rod? Will you murmur anymore? Will you complain about it anymore?

I urge you to take my text instead and read it the other way. Ask God to help you to say it:

I am glad that my God did not deliver me, because the trial has strengthened my faith. I thank His name that He has done me the great favor to allow me to carry the heavy end of His cross. I thank my Father that He has not left me without rebuke, for *before I was afflicted I went astray, but now I keep Your word* [Psalm 119:67]. *It is good for me that I was afflicted* [Psalm 119:71].

I tell you, this is the shortest way out of your troubles, as well as the most profitable attitude while you are in them. The Lord generally restrains the rod when He finds His child receiving it as a favor. When you are in agreement with God's rod, then that rod will have no further quarrel with you. When you can look into the Father's eyes and say, "Your will be done," then His afflicting hand has done its work.

**Now I come to the third point – that this trouble was permitted in order to give faith to others.**
I will address myself mainly to those who cannot say they are God's people, but who still have some desire toward Christ. It is very likely that you have had some great trouble in your life, and looking back, you wish you had never had it; but my Lord, who knows better than you do, says, "I am glad for your sakes that I did not spare you that trouble so that you might be led to believe."

Know assuredly that afflictions often lead people to faith in Christ because they have time to think. The man was strong, healthy, and hearty, and he went on working from day to day without ever thinking about God. *An ox knows its owner, and a donkey its master's manger* (Isaiah 1:3), but he did not know and did not care. He left all thoughts of eternity to those who were silly enough to be religious, but what did it matter to him? Death was a long way off, and besides, if it were not, he didn't have time to think about it. Well, an accident occurred and he had to lie upon his bed. At first he complained and was irritated, but it could not be changed, and there in the hospital room he groaned through many weary hours at night. What could he think about?

The man began to think of himself, of his condition before God, and of what his situation would be if he would die. When his life was uncertain and no one could tell which way his situation would turn, the man was forced to consider. Many souls have been plowed in the hospital and then sown in the sanctuary. Many people have been first brought to God by the loss of a limb, by long sickness, or by deep poverty.

Afflictions can often lead people to faith by preventing sin. A young man had resolved to climb a mountain. He was determined against good advice to reach the summit, even though someone much older than him had warned him of the danger. He had not proceeded far up the mountainside before a thick mist surrounded him. He was alarmed. The mist was so thick that he could hardly see his own hand. He retraced his steps, following the way by which he came. He returned sorrowfully to his father's home, telling him that he had been in great danger. His father said he was glad, for if he had not met with that danger, he might have advanced a little farther and then fallen, never to rise again.

Trouble often puts people out of temptation. They would have gone into bad company and on to drunkenness, lust, or some other sin, but they were not able to. The appointment was made. The very night was set apart, but the dark hand of God's kind angel came. I said a dark hand, for so it seemed, for the man could not do what he had wanted to do, and so his course was stopped. This was the hand of God and was the means of bringing him to faith.

Troubles often bring people to believe in Jesus because they compel them to stand face-to-face with stern realities. Did you ever lie upon the edge of death for a week? Did you ever lie with your body racked with pain, listening to the physician's whispers, knowing that there were ninety-nine chances out of a hundred that you could not possibly recover? Did you ever feel that death was near? Did you ever peer into eternity with anxious eyes? Did you ever picture hell and imagine yourself there? Did you ever lie awake thinking about heaven and seeing yourself shut out of it?

It is in such times as these that God's Holy Spirit may work great things for the children of men. Therefore Christ is glad when they are brought very low, when *their soul abhorred all kinds of food, and they drew near to the gates of death* (Psalm 107:18). It is often in their trouble that they cry unto God. Christ is glad because this is the stepping-stone to real and genuine trust in Him, and so to eternal life. It is much better to lose an eye or a hand than to lose your soul (Matthew 5:29-30). It is better to go to heaven poor and ragged than to go to hell rich. It is better to melt into heaven by the process of a slow sickness than to go down to hell with bones filled with marrow and sinews full of strength. Glory be to God for the trials and troubles some of us have had if they have been the means of bringing us to Christ.

Trials tend to make people believe in Christ when the trials are followed by deliverances. Perhaps some of you have been raised from a sick bed, or you have been helped during a time of temporal distress. Well, have you no gratitude? Do you not love God for His goodness? Does not your heart melt toward the Lord for the kind deeds He has done for you? Do you have no song of praise for His name?

I have known many who have said, "Now that God has raised me up and helped me in this way, I will give Him my heart. What can I do for Him who has done so much for me?" Gratitude, I do not doubt, has led many to put their trust in Christ. Besides, if you sought God and asked for help in time of trouble, and He did help you, this will tend to encourage you to pray again. If He helped you then, He will help you now. If He spared your life, why will He not spare your soul? If God has lifted you up from the grave, why would He not also deliver you from the pit of hell? I thank God there are many people who were led to seek the Lord through answers to prayer. God was gracious to them in their distress. His mercy listened to their prayer. The blessing came, and so they continue to cry unto Him now, and will do so as long as they live.

If we have once prevailed with God and have found some deliverance while believing in God, I hope that will cause us to trust God for everything in the future. Remember that the one thing needful for eternal life is trusting in the Lord Jesus Christ. I know you will tell me that you cannot be perfect. I know you cannot. You will say, "I have many sins. I have done much that is wrong." That is very true, but he who believes in the Lord Jesus Christ has his sins forgiven.

You know the story. Christ came down from heaven and took His people's sins upon His own shoulders. When God came forth to smite the sinner, Justice said, "Where is he?" Christ then came and stood in the sinner's place, and God's sword went through the Savior's heart. Why? So that it would never cut or wound the heart of those for whom Jesus died. Did He die for you? He did, if you believe in Him. Your faith will be the evidence to you that Christ was your substitute. If Christ suffered for you, you cannot suffer for your sins. If God punished Christ, He will never punish you. If Jesus Christ paid your debts, you are free. Before God's throne today, if you believe, you are as innocent as the angels in heaven. If you are resting upon the atonement of Christ, you are a saved soul, and you can go your way singing:

> Now free from sin, I walk at large,
> The Savior's blood's my full discharge;
> At His dear feet my soul I lay,
> A sinner saved, and homage pay.

If this is the result of your affliction, Christ may well say, "I am glad for your sakes that I was not there to stop the trouble so that you might believe." May God bring you to faith for Jesus' sake. Amen.

## Chapter 3

# Even Now

*Even now.* (John 11:22)

I hope that there are very many people here who are interested in the souls of those around them. We will certainly never exercise faith concerning those for whose salvation we have no concern. I hope, also, that we are diligent in looking after individuals, especially those who are among our own family and friends. This was what Martha did. Her whole care was for her brother. It is often easier to have faith that Christ can save sinners in general than to believe that He can come into our own home and save some particular member of our household. But, oh, the joy when this comes to pass – when we are able to kneel beside some of our loved ones and rejoice with them in being made alive by the power of the Holy Spirit!

We cannot expect to have this privilege, though, unless, like Martha, we send our prayer to Jesus, go to meet Him, and tell Him of our need. In the presence of Christ, it seems very natural to trust Him, even in the most extreme situations. It is when we are at our wits' end that He delights to help us. When our hopes seem to be buried, it is then that God can give us a resurrection. When our Isaac is on the altar, then the heavens are opened and the voice of the Eternal is heard. Are you giving way to despair concerning your dear friend? Are you beginning to doubt your Savior and to complain of His delay? You can be sure that Jesus will come at the right time, although He must be the judge of when the best time is for Him to appear.

Martha had a fine faith. If we all had as much honest belief in Christ as she had, many people who now lie dead in their sins would before long hear that voice that would call them forth from the tomb and restore them unto their friends. Martha's faith had to do with a terrible case. Her brother was dead and had been buried, but her faith still lived. In spite of all the things that went against her, she believed in Christ and looked to Him for help in her extreme situation. Her faith went to the very edge of the gulf, and she said, *Even now I know that whatever You ask of God, God will give You* (John 11:22).

Still, Martha did not have as much faith as she thought she had. Only a few hours after she had confessed her confidence in the power of the Lord Jesus, or perhaps it was only a few minutes after, she stood at the grave of her brother and evidently doubted the wisdom of Him whom she professed to trust. She objected to the stone being removed. Strong in the admitted facts of the case, she presented her reason and said, *Lord, by this time there will be a stench* (John 11:39).

But Martha, you said not very long ago, "I know that even now Christ can intervene." Yes, she said it, and she believed it in the way in which most of us believe; but when her faith was sharply tried by a matter of fact, she did not appear to have had all the faith she professed. I suspect this is also true of most of us. We often think that our confidence in Christ is much stronger than it really is.

My old friend Will Richardson, when he was seventy-five years old, said that it was a very strange thing that all winter long he thought he would like to be harvesting or working out in the hayfield because he felt so strong. He imagined that he could do as much as any of the youngsters. "But," he said, "when the summer comes, I do not get through the haymaking, and when the autumn comes, I find I do not have sufficient strength for reaping." It is often this way in spiritual things. When we are not called upon to bear the trouble, we feel wonderfully strong; but when the trial comes, very much of our boasted faith goes away as smoke. Take care that you examine your faith well. Let it be true and real, for you will need it all.

However, Christ did not take Martha at her worst, but at her best.

When our Lord says, *It shall be done to you according to your faith* (Matthew 9:29), He does not mean according to your faith in its ebb, but according to your faith in its flood. He reads the thermometer at its highest point, not at its lowest. He does not even take the average temperature of our trust. He gives us credit for our quickest pace, not our slowest, and He does not even try to use our average speed in this matter of faith. Christ did for Martha all she could have asked or believed. Her brother did rise again and was restored to her and to his friends. In your case, too, you trembling, fearful believer, the Lord Jesus will take you at your best, and He will do great things for you, for you desire to believe greatly, and your prayer is, *I do believe; help my unbelief* (Mark 9:24).

The point upon which Martha mainly rested when she expressed her faith was the power of Christ in intercession with His Father. She said, *Even now I know that whatever You ask of God, God will give You.* Since the omnipotence of God could be claimed, she felt no anxiety as to the greatness of the request. Whatever was asked could easily be gained if it was only asked by Him who never was denied.

Beloved in the Lord, our Christ is still alive, and He is still pleading. Can you believe, even now, that whatever He will ask of God will be given to Him by God, and will be given to you for His dear Son's sake? What a safe harbor the intercession of Christ is! *He is able also to save forever those who draw near to God through Him, since He always lives to make intercession for them* (Hebrews 7:25). This is a grand pillar to rest the weight of our souls upon: *He always lives to make intercession for them.*

Certainly we can have great faith in Him who never wearies and never fails. We can trust Him who lives for no other purpose than to plead for those who trust in His dying love and in His living power. *Who is the one who condemns? Christ Jesus is He who died, yes, rather who was raised, who is at the right hand of God, who also intercedes for us* (Romans 8:34). Fall back upon the intercessory power of Christ in every time of need, and you will find comfort that will never fail you.

It is a great thing to have faith for the present rather than lament the past or dream of some future faith that we hope might yet be ours. The present hour is the only time we really possess. The past is gone, and we cannot get it back. If it has been filled with faith in God, we can no more live on that faith now than we can live today on the bread we ate last week. If, on the other hand, the past has been marred by our unbelief, that is no reason why this moment could not witness a grand triumph of trust in the faithful Savior.

Let us not excuse our present lack of faith by the thought of some future blessing. No trust that we might learn to put in Christ in the days to come can atone for our present unbelief. If we ever intend to trust Him, we should do so now, since He is as worthy of our belief now as He ever will be, and since what we miss now we miss for all time.

> The present, the present is all thou hast
>     For thy sure possessing;
> Like the patriarch's angel, hold it fast
>     Till it gives its blessing.[1]

In this verse, *Even now I know that whatever You ask of God, God will give You*, I want to call your attention only to the two words *Even now*. We sometimes sing:

> Pass me not, O tender Savior!
>     Let me love and cling to Thee;
> I am longing for Thy favor;
>     When Thou comest, call for me,
>         Even me.[2]

We sing "Even me" in our hymn, and the message from the Bible text now is *Even now*. If you have been singing "Even me" and have been applying the truth to your own life, say also, with an energy of heart that will take no denial, *Even now*, and listen with earnest expectation to that gospel that is always in the present tense: *While it is said, "Today if you hear His voice, do not harden your hearts, as when they provoked Me* (Hebrews 3:15). Remember, too, that this is not only the preacher's word, for the Holy Spirit says, *Today* and *Even now*.

---

1   This is a stanza from the poem "My Soul and I" by John Greenleaf Whittier.
2   This is from Fanny Crosby's hymn "Pass Me Not, O Gentle Savior."

I will first use these words in reference to those who are concerned about the souls of others, as Martha was about her dead brother. Believe that Christ can save *even now*. Then I will speak to you who are somewhat concerned about your own souls. You believe, perhaps, that Christ can save. I want you to be convinced that He can save you *even now*; that is to say, He can save you at this exact hour and minute, while you hear these words. *Even now*, Christ can forgive. *Even now*, Christ can save. *Even now*, Christ can bless.

**First, can we believe this in regard to others?**
If you are in the same position as Martha, I can bring out several points of similarity that should encourage you to persevere. You, mother, have prayed for your boy. You, father, have pleaded for your girl. You, dear wife, have been much in prayer for your husband. You, beloved teacher, have frequently brought your class before God, and yet there is a difficult case now pressing upon your mind, and your heart is heavy about some dear child whose spiritual condition seems hopeless. I want you to believe that now, *even now*, Christ can grant your prayer and save that soul. Believe that now, *even now*, He can give you such a blessing that the past delay will be more than made up to you.

There is someone, for example, in whom we are deeply interested, and we can say that the case has cost us much sorrow. Martha could have said that about Lazarus. "Blessed Master," she might have said, "my brother has a fever, and I cared for him. I brought cold water from the well, and I wet his burning brow. I was by his bedside all night. Nobody knows how my heart was wrung with anguish as I saw the hot beaded drops upon his brow and tried to moisten his parched tongue and lips. I sorrowed as though I was about to die myself; but despite all that, I believe that *even now* You can help me; *even now*."

Sadly, there are many difficulties in the world like this. A mother says, "Nobody knows what I have suffered because of that son of mine. I will die of a broken heart because of his conduct." "No one can tell," says a father, "what grief that daughter of mine has caused me." There have been many, many such stories told to me, in which a beloved one has been the cause of anguish and agony untold to gracious, loving hearts. I speak now to those who are so grievously troubled. Can you believe that *even now* the living Intercessor is *mighty to save* (Isaiah 63:1)? It might be that you are at this moment trembling on the verge of the blessing you have sought so long. May God give you faith to grasp it *even now*!

With other people, we meet a different kind of difficulty. They have already been disappointed by the circumstances. That is how some of you have found it, is it not? "Yes," you say, "I have prayed a long time for a dear friend, and I believed some time ago that my prayer was heard and that there was a change for the better. There was an apparent change, but it came to nothing." You are just like Martha. She kept saying to herself, "Christ will come. My brother is very ill, but Jesus will come before he dies; I know He will. It cannot be that He will stay away much longer, and when He comes, Lazarus will be well." Day after day, Mary and Martha sent their messenger to look toward the Jordan River to see if Jesus was coming, but He did not come.

It must have been a terrible disappointment to both these sisters. It must have been enough to stagger the strongest faith they had ever had in the sympathy of Christ. But Martha got the better of it, and she said, "*Even now*, although I am so bitterly disappointed, I believe that You can do whatever You will." Learn from Martha, my discouraged brother. You thought that your friend was converted, but he went back again. You thought that there was a real work of grace upon his heart, but it turned out to be a mere disappointment, and it disappeared like the mist before the sun. But can you not believe above your disappointment and say, "I believe *even now*"? Your faith will be blessed if it gets that far.

Maybe we have been met by further difficulties. We have tried to help someone, and this case has proved our own helplessness. "Yes," someone says, "that describes me exactly. I have never felt so helpless in my life. I have done all that I can do, and it amounts to nothing. I have been careful in my example. I have been prayerful in my words. I have been very patient and kind. I have tried to persuade my beloved one to go and listen to the gospel here and there. I have put holy books in his way, and all the while I have seized opportunities to plead with him, often with tears in my eyes, and I can do nothing! I am exhausted."

Yes, that is just where Martha was. She had done everything, and nothing seemed to be of the least benefit. None of the medicines she applied seemed to soothe the sufferer. She had gone throughout the village, perhaps to the house of Simon the leper, who was a friend of hers, and he might have advised some new remedies – but nothing seemed to make the least difference. Her brother got worse and worse, until she saw that although she had nursed him back to health the last time he had been ill, she was now utterly powerless. Then he died. Yet even though things had gone as far as that, she had faith in Christ.

In the same way, your case is beyond your skill; but can you not believe that *even now* the end of nature will be the beginning of grace? Can you not *even now* believe that you will find that word true that He will not fail (Isaiah 42:4)? Christ has not failed yet, and He never will. When all the doctors give a patient up, the Great Physician can step in and heal. Can you believe concerning your friend *even now*?

Maybe you are in an even worse situation. The case has been given up. I think I hear a kind, gracious soul whose hope has been crushed say, "Well, sir, that is just the point we have reached with our boy. We held a little family meeting, and we said we must get him to go away to Australia, if we can. If he will only go somewhere abroad, it will be a relief to have him out of our sight. He keeps coming home intoxicated, and he gets brought before the judges. He is a disgrace to us. He is a shame to the name he bears. We have given him up."

Martha had come to this. She had given her brother up and had actually buried him, yet she believed in the power of Christ. There are many people who are buried alive! I do not know that such a thing ever happens in the cemetery, but I know it happens in our streets and homes. Many are buried morally and given up by us before God gives them up. Somehow, it is often the given-up people whom God delights to bless. Can you believe that now, *even now,* prayer can be heard, that *even now* the Holy Spirit can change the nature, and that *even now* Christ can save the soul? Do you believe this? I will rejoice if you can, and you, too, will rejoice before long.

There is still a lower depth, though. There is someone who is very concerned about an individual, and the case is terrible. "Though we loved him once," he says, "his character has now become such that it is harmful to the family. He leads others astray. We cannot think of what he has done without the very memory of his life spreading disgrace over our conscience and over our mind." There are people alive in the world who are just lumps of living corruption. There may be some reading this now. I would be glad if a word I said could reach them.

It is a shocking thing that there are men and women, made in the image of God, with talents and abilities, with capacity and conscience, who nevertheless seem to live for nothing else but to indulge their immoral passions and lead others into sins that they otherwise would not have known. There will come a dreadful day of judgment to such people when the Christ of God will sit upon the throne and will weigh before all people the secret actions and thoughts of degenerate and depraved men and women.

If any of you have someone like that related to you, can you believe that *even now* Christ can raise that person? Your situation is just the same kind that Martha had. She could have said, "My brother is buried. Even worse than that, he is decaying and stinks." She did not like to say that about dear Lazarus, her own brother, but she could not help saying it. There are some people about whom we are compelled to say, no matter how much our love seeks to shield them, that their character stinks. But can you still believe that *even now* there is hope that God can intervene and that His grace can save?

Why, my dear friend, you and I know that it is so! I believe it, and we must all believe it. If this is a situation very near and dear to you, and you begin to be a little bit doubtful, remember what you used to be yourself. You might not have been so openly depraved, perhaps, but you were inwardly quite the same. Take hope for these sinful men and women from the remembrance of what you were: *Such were some of you; but you were washed* (1 Corinthians 6:11).

When John Newton used to preach at St. Mary Woolnoth Church, he always believed in the possibility of the salvation of the worst of his hearers, for he had been himself one of the vilest of the vile. When he was very old and they said, "Dear Mr. Newton, you are too old to preach; you had better not go into the pulpit now," he said, "What! Shall the old African blasphemer, who has been saved by grace, stop preaching the gospel while there is breath in his body? Never." I think that while there is breath in our bodies, we must go on telling the gospel, for if it saved us, it can save the worst of sinners. We are bound to believe that *even now* Christ can save even the most depraved and the most vile.

> His blood can make the foulest clean,
> His blood availed for me.[3]

Maybe there is an even more desperate difficulty still, with reference to someone whom we desire to see living for God. You might think that the case is beyond our reach. "Yes," that brother quickly answers. "Now you have come to my trouble. I don't even know where my son is. He ran away, and we have not heard from him in years. How can I help him?"

Well, believe that *even now* Christ can speak to him and save him! He can send His grace where we can send our love. The great difficulty that lies like a stone at the door of the sepulcher will not prevent Him speaking the life-giving word. He has all forces at His command, and when He says the word, the stone will be rolled away. The son who is lost will be found, and the dead will be made alive again. Though you may not be able to reach your son or your daughter, Christ can meet with them. *The Lord's hand is not so short that it cannot save; nor is His ear so dull that it cannot hear* (Isaiah 59:1). Though your prodigal boy or your wandering girl may be at the end of the earth, Christ can reach them and save them. *Have faith in God* (Mark 11:22). *Even now*, Christ can help you.

> Faith, mighty faith, the promise sees,
> And looks to God alone,
> Laughs at impossibilities,
> And says, "It shall be done!"[4]

I know there are some Christian people who have drifted into the terribly wicked state of giving up their relatives as hopeless. There was a brother who is now in heaven, a good, earnest Christian man, whose son had treated him very badly indeed, and the father, justly indignant, felt it right to give his son up. He had often tried to help him, but the young man was so horribly sinful that I did not wonder that the old man turned him away. But one night as I was preaching here, I spoke

---

3   This is from Charles Wesley's hymn "O for a Thousand Tongues to Sing."
4   This is a stanza from a Charles Wesley hymn that begins with "Father of Jesus Christ, my Lord."

in the same way as I have written here, and the next morning the old man embraced his son, putting his arm around his neck. He could not help himself, but he felt that he had to go find his son and seek again to reclaim him. It seemed to have been the appointed time for that boy's salvation, for it pleased God that within a few months that son died, and he passed away with a good hope, through grace, that he had been brought to his Savior's feet by his father's love.

If any of you have a very bad son, go seeking after him until, by the grace of God, you find him. And you who have grown hopeless about your relatives, you must try not to give up on them. If other people cast them off, you must not, for they are connected to you by the ties of blood. Seek them out. You are the best person in the world to seek them, and the most likely to find them – if you can believe that *even now*, when the worst has come to the worst, *even now* almighty grace can step in and save the lost soul.

Oh, that some here might have faith to claim at this moment the salvation of their friends! May desire be worked into expectancy, and hope become certainty! Like Jacob at Jabbok, may we lay hold of God, saying, *I will not let You go unless You bless me* (Genesis 32:26). To such faith, the Lord will give a quick response. He who will not be denied shall not be denied. My friend Hudson Taylor, who has done such a wonderful work for China, is an example of this. Brought up in a godly home, he, as a young man, tried to imitate the lives of his parents. Failing in his own strength to make himself better, he swung to the other extreme and began to entertain skeptical notions. One day when his mother was away from home, a great yearning after her boy consumed her, and she went up to her room to plead with God that *even now* He would save him. If I remember right, she said that she would not leave the room until she had the assurance that her boy would be brought to Christ.

At length her faith triumphed, and she rose quite certain that all was well, and that *even now* her son was saved. What was he doing at that time? Having half an hour to spare, he wandered into his father's library and aimlessly took down one book after another to find some short and interesting passage to divert his mind. He could not find what he wanted in any of the books, so seeing a narrative tract, he took it up with the intention of reading the story, intending to put it down when the sermon part of it began. As he read, he came to the words "the finished work of Christ," and almost at the very moment in which his mother, who was miles away, claimed his soul for God, light came into his heart. He saw that it was by the finished work of Christ that he was to be saved, and kneeling in his father's library, he sought and found the life of God.

Some days later, after his mother returned, Hudson said to her, "I have some news to tell you."

"Oh, I know what it is!" she answered, smiling. "You have given yourself to God."

"Who told you?" he asked in astonishment.

"God told me," she said, and together they praised Him who at the same moment had given the faith to the mother and the life to the son, and who has since made him such a blessing to the world. It was the mother's faith, claiming the blessing *even now* that did it.

I tell you this remarkable incident so that many others might be stirred up to the same immediate and urgently persistent desire for the salvation of their children and relatives. There are some things we must always pray for with submission as to whether it is the will of God to give to us, but we can ask for the salvation of men and women without any fear. God delights to save and to bless, and when the faith is given to us to expect an immediate answer to such a prayer, thrice happy are we. Seek such faith *even now*, I urge you – *even now*.

**Next, I want to speak very earnestly to any here who are concerned about their own souls.**

Jesus can save you *even now*. Can we believe this for ourselves? Can you expect the Lord, even while you hear these words, to speak the word of power to you and bring you forth from your sleep of sin?

For some of you, the time is late – very late – yet it is not too late. You are getting up in years, my friend, but I want you to believe that *even now* Christ can save you. I often notice the number of old people who come to the Tabernacle.[5] I am glad to see the aged saints, but among so many elderly people, there are no doubt some unsaved sinners whose grey hairs are not a crown of glory (Proverbs 16:31), but a fool's cap.

---

5   This refers to the London Metropolitan Tabernacle, where Charles Spurgeon pastored.

But however old you are, whether you are sixty, seventy, eighty, or even ninety years of age, yet *even now* Christ can give you life. Blessed be God for that!

It is not entirely the years that trouble you, though, but it is your sins. As I have already said, even if you have gone to the very extremity of sin, you can believe that, after all these years of wandering, the arms of free grace are still open to receive you *even now*. There is an old proverb that "It is never too late to mend." It is always too late for us to mend ourselves, but it is never too late for Christ to mend us. Christ can make us new, and it is never too late for Him to do so. If you come to Him and trust Him, He will receive you *even now*.

By the kind patience of God, there might be time left to you in which you may turn to Him. What a thousand mercies it is that *even now* is a time of mercy to you, for it could have been the moment of your everlasting doom! You have had accidents. You have been within an inch of the grave many times. You have been ill, seriously ill. You have been nearly given up for dead, and here you are still alive – and still an enemy to God! You were plucked by His hand from fire and flood, and perhaps from battle. You were delivered from fever and disease, and yet you are still ungrateful, still rebelling, and still spending the life that grace has lent you in resisting the love of God! You should have believed in Christ many years ago, but the text says, *even now*.

Do not begin to say, "I believe God could have saved me years ago." There is no faith in that. Do not meet my earnest plea by saying, "I believe that God can save me under certain conditions." Believe that He can save you now just as you are. You came in here careless and thoughtless, yet *even now* He can save you. You might be quite a man of the world, free and easy, absent of all religious inclinations, but He can save you *even now*.

*O God, strike many people down, as You did with Saul of Tarsus, and change their hearts by Your own supreme love, as You can do even now on the very spot where they are!*

But although God waits to be gracious to you, and although you may still have time to repent, remember that it is only time; therefore, seize it. Your opportunity will not last forever. I believe that even now God can save, but if you reject Christ, there will come a time when salvation will be impossible. On earth, as long as someone desires to be saved, he may be saved. While there is life, there is hope. I believe that if a person could look to Christ even as his breath were going from his body, he would live. But:

> There are no acts of pardon passed
>     In the cold grave to which we haste;
> But darkness, death, and long despair,
>     Reign in eternal silence there.[6]

Do not set out on that last leap without Christ, but *even now*, before the clock strikes another hour, run to Jesus. Trust Him *even now*.

It is still a time of hope. *Even now*, there is still every opportunity and every preparation for the sinner's salvation. *Behold, now is "the acceptable time," behold, now is "the day of salvation"* (2 Corinthians 6:2). I will give you some reasons for believing that *even now* is a time of hope. There are many good arguments that can be brought out in order to drive out any thoughts of despair.

First, the gospel is still preached. The old-fashioned gospel is not dead yet. There are very many people who would like to muzzle the mouths of God's ministers, but they never will. The old gospel will live when they are dead, and because it is still preached to you, you can still believe and live.

What is the old gospel? It is Christ coming to restore you, or to bring you back to God, because you were helpless to save yourself. It is Jesus Christ taking those sins of yours, which were enough to sink you to hell, and bearing them on the cross so that He might bring you to heaven. If you will only trust Him, *even now*, He will deliver you from the curse of the law, for it is written, *He that believeth on him is not condemned* (John 3:18 KJV). If you will trust Him, *even now*, He will give you a life of blessedness that will never end, for again it is written, *He who believes in the Son has eternal life* (John 3:36).

Because that gospel is preached, there is hope for you. When there is no hope, there will be no presentation of the gospel. God must, by a

---

[6] This is a stanza from Isaac Watts' hymn that begins with "Life is the time to serve the Lord."

command, suspend the preaching of the gospel before He can suspend the fulfilment of the gospel promise to everyone who believes. Since there is a gospel, take it. Take it now – *even now*. May God help you to do so!

Second, I know there is hope now, *even now*, for Christ still lives. He rose from the dead, no more to die, and He is as strong as ever. He said, *I was dead, and behold, I am alive forevermore* (Revelation 1:18). Those words were spoken to the apostle John, and when he saw Him, he said, *His head and His hair were white like white wool, like snow* (Revelation 1:14). However, when the spouse saw Him, she said, *His locks are like clusters of dates and black as a raven* (Song of Solomon 5:11). Yet both saw clearly.

John's vision of the white hair was to show that Christ is the Ancient of Days (Daniel 7:9), but the view of the spouse was to show His everlasting youth and His unceasing strength and power to save. If there is any difference in Him, Christ is today more mighty to save than He was when Martha saw Him. He had not then completed the work of our salvation, but He has perfectly accomplished it now, and therefore there is hope for everyone who trusts in Him. My Lord has gone up beyond where a prayer will find Him, with the keys of death and hell hanging at his belt (Revelation 1:18), and with the omnipotence of God in His right hand. If you believe on Him, by His eternal power and Godhead (Romans 1:20), He will save you. He will save you *even now*, right now, before you leave this place.

Third, I know that this is a time of hope because the precious blood still has power. All salvation is through the blood of the Lamb. It remains true:

> There is a fountain filled with blood,
>     Drawn from Immanuel's veins;

and still, *even now*:

> And sinners, plunged beneath that flood,
>     Lose all their guilty stains.[7]

---

[7] These lines (and the stanza a few lines later) are from William Cowper's hymn "There Is a Fountain Filled with Blood."

The endless effectiveness of the atoning sacrifice is the reason why you may come and believe in Jesus *even now*. If that blood had diminished in its force, I would not dare to speak as I do; but I can *even now* say with confidence:

> Dear dying Lamb, Thy precious blood
>    Shall never lose its power,
> Till all the ransomed church of God
>    Be saved to sin no more.

How many have already entered into glory by the blood of the Lamb! When someone comes to die, nothing else will do for him but the blood of the Lamb. Our own works are a poor staff for us when we pass through the river. All those who are now in the land of light have only one confidence and only one song: they stand upon the merit of Jesus Christ, and they praise the Lamb who was slain, by whose blood they have been cleansed and sanctified. There is no other way of salvation except that. *Even now* that blood has virtue to take away your sin. Christ is a sufficient Savior because His death has inexhaustible power. Believe that He can save you *even now*.

Fourth, *even now* is a time of hope to you because the Spirit can still renew. He is still at work regenerating and sanctifying. He came down at Pentecost to dwell with His people, and He has never gone back again. He is still in the church. Sometimes we feel His mighty power more than at other times, but He is always at work. Oh, you who do not know anything about the power of the Holy Spirit, let me tell you that this is the most wonderful phenomenon that can ever be observed! Those of us who have seen and known His mighty power can bear testimony to it.

In my time of rest at Menton during the last few weeks, if you had seen me, you would have found me sitting every morning at half-past nine at my little table with my Bible, just reading a chapter and offering prayer – my family prayer with the little group of from forty to fifty friends who gathered daily for that morning act of worship. There they met, and the Spirit of God was clearly moving among them converting, cheering, and comforting. It was not because of any effort of mine. It was simply the Word, attended by the Spirit of God, binding us together and binding us all to Christ.

And here in this place for thirty-seven years, I have in all simplicity preached this old-fashioned gospel. I have simply kept to that one theme. I was content to know nothing else among men. Where are those who have preached new gospels? They have been like the mist upon the mountain's brow. They came, and they have gone. It will always be that way with those who preach anything else but the Word of God, for nothing will abide except the mountain itself – the everlasting truth of the gospel to which the Holy Spirit bears witness. That same Holy Spirit is able to give you a new heart *even now* in order to make you a new creature in Christ Jesus at this moment. *Do you believe this?* (John 11:26).

Fifth, I know that Christ can save you *even now*, and I pray that you will believe it, for the Father is still waiting to receive returning prodigals. Still, as of old, the door is open, and the best robe hangs in the hall ready to be put upon the shoulders of the son who comes back from the far country, even if he returns reeking with the stench of the swine trough. How longingly the Father looks along the road to see whether at last some of you are turning homeward (Luke 15:20)! If you only knew the joy that awaits those who come, and the feast that would fill the welcoming table, you would *even now* say, *I will get up and go to my Father* (Luke 15:18). You should have returned long ago, but blessed be His love that *even now* waits to hold you close to His heart!

Finally, Jesus Christ can save you *even now*, for faith is but the work of a moment. Believe and live (John 11:25). You do not have to do anything. You do not need any preparations. Come as you are, without a single plea except that He calls you to come.[8] Come now – *even now*.

If Christ were far away, the time that is left to some of you might be too short to reach Him. If there were many things that you had to do first, your life might end before they were half done. If faith had to grow strong before it resulted in salvation, you might be in the place of eternal despair before your faith had time to be more than a mere mustard seed. However, Christ is not far away. He is in our midst. He is by your side. You do not have to do anything before you trust Him, for He has done it all. However weak your faith may be, if it simply comes

---

8   See Charlotte Elliott's hymn "Just as I Am."

in contact with Christ, it will impart instant blessing to you. *Even now* you can be saved for ever.

> The moment a sinner believes,
>     And trusts in his crucified God,
> His pardon at once he receives,
>     Redemption in full through His blood.[9]

Certainly these are all sufficient reasons why *even now* is a time of hope to you. May it also be a time of blessing! It will be so if you will only at this moment cast yourself on Christ. He says to you that if you will only believe, *you will see the glory of God* (John 11:40). Martha saw that glory. You will see it, too, if you have the same precious faith (2 Peter 1:1). I desire that God would give me some souls today. I desire earnestly that He would set the bells of heaven ringing because sinners have returned and heirs of glory have been born into the family of grace. I urged you earlier to pray. Pray mightily that this word, simple but direct, would be blessed to many *even now*.

---

[9] This is from Joseph Hart's hymn that begins with "The moment a sinner believes."

## Chapter 4

# Though He Were Dead

*Martha saith unto him, I know that he shall rise again in the resurrection at the last day. Jesus said unto her, I am the resurrection, and the life: he that believeth in me, though he were dead, yet shall he live: and whosoever liveth and believeth in me shall never die. Believest thou this?* (John 11:24-26 KJV)

Martha is a very accurate type of a class of anxious believers. They really do believe, but not with such confidence as to lay aside their worry. They do not distrust the Lord or question the truth of what He says, yet they wonder in their minds things like, "How will this thing happen?" and so they miss the major part of the present comfort that the word of the Lord would minister to their hearts if they received it more simply. *How* and *why* belong to the Lord. It is His business to arrange matters so as to fulfil His own promises. If we would sit at our Lord's feet with Mary and consider what He has promised, we would choose a better part than if we ran around with Martha crying, "How can these things be?"

In this case, when the Lord Jesus Christ told Martha that her brother would rise again, she replied, *I know that he will rise again in the resurrection on the last day* (John 11:24). She was a type of certain anxious believers, for she set a practical limit to the Savior's words: "Of course there will be a resurrection, and then my brother will rise with the rest." She concluded that the Savior could not mean anything more than that. The first and most common meaning that suggests itself to her must be what Jesus means. Is not that the way with many of us?

We had a statesman once who was a good man and who loved reform, but whenever he had achieved a little progress, he considered that the work was all done. We eventually called him "Finality John," for he was always coming to the end of something. He took for his motto "Rest, and be thankful." Christians are often the same way in regard to the promises of God. We limit the Holy One of Israel as to the meaning of His words. We know that the words mean a certain thing, but we do not think they can mean anything more. It would be good if the spirit of progress would enter into our faith so that we felt within our souls that we had never beheld the innermost glory of the Lord's words of grace.

We are often amazed that the disciples put such poor meanings upon our Lord's words, but I fear we are almost as far off as they were from fully comprehending all His gracious teachings. Are we not still like little children, making little out of great words? Have we yet grasped even a tenth of our Lord's full meaning in many of His sayings of love? When He is talking about bright and sparkling gems of benediction, we think of common pebbles in the brook of mercy. When He speaks of stars and heavenly crowns, we think of sparks and children's garlands made of fading flowers. Oh, that we could have our intellect cleared; better still, it would be good if we could have our understanding expanded. Best of all, it would be good to have our faith increased so as to reach to the height of our Lord's great arguments of love!

Martha also had another fault in which she was very like us: she set the words of Jesus on the shelf as things so ordinary and common that they were of little practical importance. *Your brother will rise again* (John 11:23). If Martha had possessed enough faith, she might truthfully have said, "Lord, I thank You for that word! I expect within a short space to see him sitting at the table with You. I put the best meaning possible upon Your words, for I know that You are always better than I can imagine You to be. Therefore, I expect to see my beloved Lazarus walk home from the sepulcher before the sun sets again." But no, she laid the truth aside as a matter past all dispute, saying, *I know that he will rise again in the resurrection on the last day.*

A great many precious truths are laid aside by us like old vehicles in the junkyard, never to see service any more, or like aged pensioners cast aside as relics of the past. We say, "Yes, that is quite true. We fully believe that doctrine." Somehow it is almost as bad to cover up a doctrine in lavender as it is to throw it out the window. When you so believe a truth as to put it to bed and cover it with the blanket of neglect, it is much the same as if you did not believe it at all. An official belief is very much related to unbelief.

Some people never question a doctrine. They are not even tempted to do so. They accept the gospel as true, but then they never expect to see its promises practically carried out. They see it as a proper thing to believe, but by no means do they see it as a prominent, practical factor in actual life. It is true, but it is mysterious, cloudy, mythical, and far removed from the realm of practical common sense.

We often do the same with the promises as a poor old couple did with a precious document that might have cheered their old age if they had used it according to its real value. A gentleman entered a poor woman's house and saw framed upon the wall a French note for a thousand francs. He said to the old folks, "How did you get this?" They informed him that a poor French soldier had been taken in by them and nursed until he died, and he had given them that little picture when he was dying as a memorial of him. They thought it was such a pretty souvenir that they had framed it, and there it was adorning the cottage wall. They were greatly surprised when they were told that it was worth a sum that would be quite a little fortune for them if they would simply turn it into money.

Are we not equally impractical with far more precious things? Have you not taken certain words of your great Lord and framed them in your hearts? You say to yourselves, "They are so sweet and precious," and yet you have never turned them into an actual blessing. You have never used them in the hour of need. You have done as Martha did when she took the words, *Your brother will rise again,* and put them in a nice frame that said, *in the resurrection on the last day.* Oh, that we had grace to turn God's bullion of gospel into coins and use them as our present spending money!

Moreover, Martha made another mistake, and that was setting the promise in the far-off distance. Distancing the promises of the Most High is a common problem. *In the resurrection on the last day.* No doubt Martha thought it was a very long way off, and therefore she did not get much comfort out of it. Telescopes are meant to bring objects near to the eye, but I have known people to use mental telescopes the wrong way. They always put the big end of it to their eye, and then the mirror makes the object seem farther away.

Martha's brother was to be raised that very day. She could have understood the Savior that way, but instead she looked at His words through the wrong end of the telescope and said, *I know that he will rise again in the resurrection on the last day.* Brethren, do not refuse the present blessing. Death and heaven, or the second coming and the glory, are at your doors. *In a very little while, He who is coming will come, and will not delay* (Hebrews 10:37). *The Lord is not slow about His promise* (2 Peter 3:9). Do not say in your heart that your Lord delays His coming (Matthew 24:48). Do not think that His words of love are only for the distant future. In the ages to come, marvels will be revealed, but even the present hour is adorned with loving-kindness. Today the Lord has rest, peace, and joy to give to you. Do not lose these treasures by unbelief.

Martha also seems to me to have made the promise unreal and impersonal. *Your brother will rise again*: to have realized that would have been a great comfort to her, but she mixed Lazarus up with all the rest of the dead. "Yes, *he will rise again in the resurrection on the last day.* When thousands of millions will be rising from their graves, no doubt Lazarus will rise with the rest." We are the same way. We take the promise and say, "This is true for all the children of God." If so, it is true for us – but we miss that point.

What a blessing God has bestowed upon the covenanted people! Yes, you are one of them, but you shake your head as if the word was not for you. It is a fine feast, and yet you are hungry. It is a full and flowing stream, but you remain thirsty. Why is this? Somehow your general understanding misses the sweetness that comes from personal application. There is such a thing as speaking of the promises in a magnificent style, and yet being in deep spiritual poverty. It is as if a man should boast of the wealth of his nation and the vast amount of treasure in the bank, while he does not own even a penny of it himself.

In your case, you know it is your own fault that you are poor and miserable, for if you would only exercise the proper faith, you could possess an unlimited inheritance. If you are a child of God, all things are yours and you can help yourself. If you are hungry at this banquet, it is because of lack of faith. If you are thirsty by the bank of this river, it is because you do not bend down and drink. Behold, God is your portion (Lamentations 3:24). The Father is your shepherd, the Son of God is your food, and the Spirit of God is your comforter. Rejoice and be glad, and with the firm hand of a personal faith grasp that royal blessing that Jesus sets before you in His promises.

I urge you to observe how the Lord Jesus Christ in great wisdom dealt with Martha. In the first place, He did not grow angry with her. There is not a trace of irritation in His speech. He did not say to her, "Martha, I am ashamed of you that you would have such low thoughts of Me." She thought that she was honoring Jesus when she said, *Even now I know that whatever You ask of God, God will give You* (John 11:22). Her idea of Jesus was that He was a great prophet who would ask God and obtain answers to His prayers. She had not grasped the truth of His own personal power to give and sustain life. But the Savior did not say, "Martha, these are low and poor ideas of your Lord and Savior." He did not rebuke her, even though she lacked wisdom that she should have possessed.

I don't think God's people learn much by being scolded. It is not the habit of the great Lord to scold His disciples, and therefore they do not take it well when His servants take it upon themselves to rebuke them. If ever you meet with one of the Lord's own followers who falls far short of the true ideal of the gospel, do not rant and scold. Who taught you what you know? He who has taught you did it out of His infinite love and grace and compassion. He was very tender with you, for you were ignorant enough. Therefore, be tender and patient with others, just as your Lord was gentle toward you. It is not proper for a servant to lose patience where his Master shows so much.

With a gentle spirit, the Lord Jesus proceeded to teach Martha more of the things concerning Himself. More of Jesus! More of Jesus! That is the sovereign cure for our faults. He revealed Himself to her so that in Him she could see reasons for a clearer hope and a more substantial faith. How sweetly those words fell upon her ear: *I am the resurrection and the life* (John 11:25). He did not say, "I can get resurrection by My prayers," but, "I Myself am the resurrection."

God's people need to know more of what Jesus is, more of the fulness that it has pleased the Father to place in Him. Some of them know well enough what they are themselves, and they will break their hearts if they go on reading much longer only from that depressing book. They need to rest their eyes upon the person of their Lord. They need to learn about all the riches of grace that lie hidden in Him. Then they will gain courage and will look forward with more certain expectation. When our Lord said, *I am the resurrection and the life*, He indicated to Martha that resurrection and life were not gifts that He had to seek, nor even blessings that He had to create, but that He Himself was the resurrection and the life. These things were wherever He was. He was the author, giver, and maintainer of life – and that life was Himself. He wanted Martha to know that He Himself was precisely what she needed for her brother. She did know a little of the Lord's power, for she said, *Lord, if You had been here, my brother would not have died* (John 11:21), which could mean, "Lord, You are the life."

"Yes," Jesus said, "but you must also learn that I am the resurrection! You already admit that if I had been here, Lazarus would not have died, but I also want you to learn that with Me here, your brother will live even though he has died (John 11:25). I want you to know that when I am with My people, none of them will die forever, for I am to them the resurrection and the life." Poor Martha was looking up into the sky for life, or gazing down into the deeps for resurrection, when the Resurrection and the Life stood before her, smiling upon her, and comforting her heavy heart. She had thought of what Jesus might have done if He had been there before, but she needed to know what He is at the present moment.

I have introduced the text to you, and I pray God the Holy Spirit to bless these introductory observations. If we learn only these first lessons, we will not have read in vain. Let us understand promises in their largest sense, let us regard them as real, and let us set them down as facts. Let us look to the Promiser, even to Jesus the Lord, and not look as much to the difficulties that surround the accomplishment of the promise. In beginning the divine life, let us look to Jesus, and later in running the heavenly race, let us still be looking unto Jesus until we see in Him our all in all. When both eyes look upon Jesus, we are in the light; but when we have one eye on Him and one eye on self, all is darkness. Oh, to see Him with all our soul's eyes!

Now I am going to speak as I am helped by the Spirit, and I will proceed by first asking you to view the text as a stream of comfort to Martha and other bereaved people, and then to view it as a great source of comfort to all believers.

### First, I want you to view the text as a stream of comfort to Martha and other bereaved people.

Observe in the beginning that the presence of Jesus Christ means life and resurrection. It meant that to Lazarus. If Jesus comes to Lazarus, Lazarus must live. If Martha had taken the Savior's words literally, as she should have done, she would have had immediate comfort from them – and the Savior intended her to understand them in that sense. He basically says, "I am the Power that can make Lazarus live again. I am the Power that can keep him in life. Yes, *I am the resurrection and the life.*"

A statement understood this way would have been very comfortable to Martha. Nothing could have been more comforting. It would then and there have abolished death as far as her brother was concerned. Somebody says, "But I do not see how this is any comfort to us, for if Jesus is here, it is only a spiritual presence, and we cannot expect to see our dear mother or child or husband raised from the dead by that." I answer that our Lord Jesus is able at this moment to give us back our departed ones, for He is still the resurrection and the life.

But let me ask you whether you really would want Jesus to raise your departed ones from the dead. At first you say, "Of course I do," but I would ask you to reconsider that decision. I believe that upon further consideration you will say, "No, I could not want that." Do you really want to see your glorified husband sent back again to this world of care and pain? Would you want your father or mother deprived of the glories that they are now enjoying in order that they might help you in the struggles of this mortal life? Would you take the crown away from the saints? You are not that cruel. Would you really want that dear child back from among the angels and from the inner glory to come here and suffer again? You would not want it so.

To my mind it is, or should be, a comfort to you that it is not within your power to have your departed loved one back because you might be tempted in some selfish moment to accept the doubtful blessing. Lazarus could return and fit into his place again, but scarcely one in ten thousand could do so. There would be serious drawbacks in the return of those whom we have loved best.

Do you cry, "Give back my father! Give me back my friend"? You do not know what you ask. It might be a cause of regret to you as long as they remained here, for you would think to yourself every day, "Beloved one, I have brought you out of heaven by my wish. I have robbed you of infinite joy in order to gratify myself." As for me, I would rather have the Lord Jesus keep the keys of death than that He should lend them to me. It would be too dreadful a privilege to be empowered to rob heaven of the perfected merely to give pleasure to imperfect ones below. Jesus would raise them now if He knew it was right. I do not want to take the government from His shoulder (Isaiah 9:6). It is more comfortable to me to think that Jesus Christ could give them back to me, and He would do so if it were for His glory and my good.

My dear ones who lie asleep could be awakened in an instant if the Master thought it best; but it would not be best, and therefore even I would say, "Tread softly, Master! Do not awake them! I will go to them, but they will not return to me [2 Samuel 12:23]. It is not my wish for them to return. It is better that they should be with You where You are and behold Your glory." It does not seem to me, then, dear friend, that you are one bit behind Martha. You should be comforted while Jesus says to you, "I am even now the resurrection and the life."

Here is more comfort that we can each safely take: when Jesus comes, the dead will live. *He who believes in Me will live even if he dies* (John 11:25). We do not know when our Lord will descend from heaven, but we do know the message of the angel: *This Jesus, who has been taken up from you into heaven, will come in just the same way as you have watched Him go into heaven* (Acts 1:11). The Lord will come. We may not question the certainty of His appearing. When He comes, all His redeemed will live with Him. The trump of the archangel will startle the happy sleepers, and they will wake to put on their beautiful garments (1 Thessalonians 4:16). The body will be transformed and will be made like unto Christ's glorious body (Philippians 3:21), and will be once more wrapped around them as the garment of their perfected and emancipated spirits. Then our brother will rise again, and the Lord will bring with Him all our dear ones who have fallen asleep in Jesus. This is the glorious hope of the church, wherein we see the death of death and the destruction of the grave. *Therefore comfort one another with these words* (1 Thessalonians 4:18).

We are also told that when Jesus comes, living believers will not die. After the coming of Christ, there will be no more death for His people. What does Paul say? *Behold, I tell you a mystery; we will not all die, but we will all be changed* (1 Corinthians 15:51). Did I see a little schoolgirl raise her hand? Did I hear her say, "Please, sir, you made a mistake." So I did; I made it on purpose. Paul did not say, *We will not all die*, for the Lord had already said, *Everyone who lives and believes in Me will never die* (John 11:26). Paul would not say that any of us would die, but he used his Master's own term, and said, *We will not all sleep, but we will all be changed.*

When the Lord comes, there will be no more death. Those who are alive and remain (1 Thessalonians 4:17) will undergo a sudden transformation, for flesh and blood cannot inherit the kingdom of God, and by that transformation our bodies will be made ready to *share in the inheritance of the saints in light* (Colossians 1:12). There will be no more death then.

Therefore, we have two sacred handkerchiefs with which to wipe the eyes of mourners: (1) when Christ comes the dead will live, and (2) when Christ comes, those who live will never die. Like Enoch or Elijah, we will pass into the glorious condition without wading through the black stream, while those who have already forded it will prove to have not lost anything by having done so. All this is in connection with Jesus. Resurrection with Jesus is resurrection indeed. Life in Jesus is life indeed. When we see resurrection, glory, eternal life, and ultimate perfection coming to us in Jesus, they are all endeared to us. Jesus is the golden pot that has this manna, the rod that bears these almonds, and the life whereby we live.

But I have not made you drink deeply enough from this stream yet. I think our Savior meant that even now His dead are alive. *He who believes in Me will live even if he dies.* Those who believe in Jesus Christ appear to die, but yet they live. They are not in the grave, but they are forever with the Lord. They are not unconscious, but they are with their Lord in paradise. Death cannot kill a believer; it can only usher him into a freer form of life. Because Jesus lives, His people live. God is *not the God of the dead, but of the living* (Mark 12:27). Those who have departed have not perished. We laid the precious body in the cemetery and we set up a headstone, but we could engrave on them the Lord's words, *She has not died, but is asleep* (Luke 8:52). It is true that an unbelieving generation might laugh us to scorn, but we scorn their laughing.

Even now, His living do not die. There is an essential difference between the death of the godly and the death of the ungodly. Death comes to the ungodly person as a matter of punishment and judgment, but to the righteous as a call to his Father's palace. To the sinner, it is an execution; to the saint, it is a revelation. Death to the wicked is the king of terrors; death to the saint is the end of terrors and the beginning of glory. To die in the Lord is a covenant blessing (Revelation 14:13). Death is ours. It is written down in the list of our possessions among the *all things* (2 Corinthians 6:10), and it follows life in the list as if it were an equal blessing. It no longer means death for us to die. The name remains, but the thing itself is changed.

Why, then, are we in bondage through fear of death? Why do we dread the process that gives us liberty? I am told that people who in the cruel ages had lain in prison for years suffered much more in the moment when their chains were knocked off than they had endured for months in wearing the hard iron; yet I suppose that no one languishing in a dungeon would have been unwilling to stretch out his arm or leg so that the heavy chains could be beaten off by the blacksmith.

We should all be content to endure that little inconvenience in order to obtain lasting liberty. Knocking off the fetters is like death, yet the iron may never seem to be so truly iron as when that last liberating blow of grace is about to fall. Let us not mind the harsh grating of the key as it turns in the lock. If we understand it properly, it will be as music to our ears. Imagine that your last hour is come! The key turns with pain for a moment, but then the lock is opened. The iron gate opens! The spirit is free! Glory be unto the Lord forever and ever!

**Now I want you to look at the text and see it as a great source of comfort for all believers.**
I cannot understand it any more than I could measure the bottomless pit, but I can invite you to survey it with the help of the Holy Spirit.

First, this text plainly teaches that the Lord Jesus Christ is the life of His people. We are dead by nature, and you can never produce life out of death, for the essential elements are lacking. If a spark is lingering among the ashes, you might still be able to fan it into a flame; but the last spark of heavenly life is gone from human nature, and it is vain to seek for life among the dead. The life of every Christian is Christ. He is the beginning of life, being the Resurrection. When He comes to us, we live. Regeneration is the result of contact with Christ. We are born again unto a living hope by His resurrection from the dead. The life of the Christian in its beginning is in Christ alone. Not a fragment of it is from ourselves, and the continuance of that life is just the same. Jesus is not only the resurrection to begin with, but He is the life to continue with. Some people might think that they have life in themselves, but we have no spiritual life other than life as it is in Christ. Every breath that your spiritual life draws is in Christ. If you are regarded for a moment as separated from Christ, you are cast forth as a branch and are withered.

A part of the body severed from the head is dead flesh and is no more. Your life is in union to Christ. Oh, that our hearers would understand this! I see a poor sinner look into himself, and look again, and then cry, "I cannot see any life within!" Of course you cannot; you do not have any life of your own.

A Christian cries out, "I cannot find anything within to feed my soul!" Do you expect to feed upon yourself? Must not Israel look up for the manna? Did any of the tribes of Israel find the manna in their own tents? To look to self is to turn to a broken cistern that cannot hold any water (Jeremiah 2:13). You must learn that Jesus is the resurrection and the life. Listen to that great "I" – that infinite I! This must cover over and swallow up your little I – your little ego. *It is no longer I who live, but Christ lives in me* (Galatians 2:20).

What are you? We are less than nothing, and vanity, but over it all springs up that divine, all-sufficient personality: *I am the resurrection and the life.* Take the first two words together, and they seem to me to have a wondrous majesty about them: *I am.* This is self-existence. There is life in Himself. Even as the Mediator, the Lord Jesus tells us that it is given to Him to have life in Himself, even as the Father has life in Himself (John 5:26). *I am* fills the yawning mouth of the sepulcher. He who lives and was dead and is alive for evermore, the Alpha and the Omega, the beginning and the end (Revelation 1:18; 22:13), declares, *I am the resurrection and the life.*

If, then, I want to live unto God, I must have Christ. If I desire to continue to live unto God, I must continue to have Christ. If I aspire to have that life developed to the utmost fulness of which it is capable, I must find it all in Christ. He has come not only that we might have life, but that we might have it more abundantly (John 10:10). Anything that is beyond the circle of Christ is death. If I dream up an experience over which I foolishly gloat, and it fills me with such pride that I do not see my need to come to Christ now as a poor empty-handed sinner, I have entered into the realm of death and have introduced into my soul a damning leaven. Away with it! Away with it! Everything of life is put into this golden casket of Christ Jesus; everything else is death. We do not have a breath of life anywhere but in Jesus, who lives always to give life. He said, *Because I live, you will live also* (John 14:19), and this is true. We do not live for any other reason. It is not because of anything in us or connected with us, but only because of Jesus. *For you have died and your life is hidden with Christ in God* (Colossians 3:3).

Even further in this great source to which we would guide you, faith is the only means by which we can draw our life from Jesus. *I am the resurrection and the life; he who believes in Me.* That is it. Jesus does not say, "He who loves Me," even though love is the greatest commandment (Matthew 22:37) and is very sweet to God. He does not say, "He who serves Me," even though everyone who believes in Christ will labor to serve Him. He does not even say, "He who imitates Me," even though everyone who believes in Christ must and will imitate Him. Rather, Jesus said, *He who believes in Me.*

Why is that? Why does the Lord so continually make faith to be the only link between Himself and the soul? As I understand it, it is because faith is a grace that claims nothing to itself and has no operation apart from Jesus, to whom it unites us. If you want to conduct electricity, you must find a metal that will not create any action of its own. If it did so, it would disturb the current that you want to send along it. If it set up an action of its own, how would you know the difference between what came from the metal and what came from the battery? Faith is an empty-handed receiver and communicator. It is nothing apart from that upon which it relies, and therefore it is suitable to be a conductor for grace.

When an auditorium has to be built so that a speaker can be plainly heard, the essential thing is to get rid of all echo. When you have no echo, then you have a perfect building. Faith makes no noise of its own. It allows the Word to speak. Faith cries, "Not to us! Not to us!" (Psalm 115:1). Christ puts His crown on faith's head, exclaiming, *Your faith has saved you* (Luke 7:50), but faith hastens to ascribe all the glory of salvation to Jesus only.

The Lord selects faith rather than any other grace because it is a self-forgetting thing. It is best adapted to be the conduit through which the water of life runs because it will not impart a flavor of its own, but will just convey the stream purely and simply from Christ to the soul. *He who believes in Me.*

Notice that there is no limit to the reception of Christ by faith. *He that believeth in me, though he were dead, yet shall he live: and whosoever . . .* (John 11:25-26 KJV). I am deeply in love with that word *whosoever*. It is a splendid word. A person who kept many animals had some large dogs and some little ones, and in his eagerness to let them enter his house freely he had two holes cut in the door – one for the large dogs and another for the little dogs. You may well laugh, for the little dogs could surely have come in wherever there was room for the larger ones. This *whosoever* is the large opening, suitable for sinners of every size.

*Whosoever liveth and believeth in me shall never die* (John 11:26 KJV). Does anyone have a right to believe in Christ? The gospel gives every person the right to believe in Christ, for we are commanded to preach it to everyone, with this command: *Listen, that you may live* (Isaiah 55:3). Everyone has a right to believe in Christ, because he will be damned if he does not; and he must have a right to do that which will bring him into condemnation if he does not do it. It is written, *He that believeth and is baptized shall be saved; but he that believeth not shall be damned* (Mark 16:16 KJV). That makes it clear that I, whoever I may be, since I have a right to try to escape from damnation, have a right to avail myself of the blessed command, *Believe in the Lord Jesus, and you will be saved* (Acts 16:31). Oh, that *whosoever*, that hole in the door for the large dog! Do not forget it!

Come and put your trust in Christ. If you can only get united with Christ, you are a living person. If only your finger touches the hem of His garment, you are made whole (Luke 8:43-44). You only need the touch of faith, and the virtue flows from Him to you – and He is to you the resurrection and the life.

I want you to notice that there is no limit to this power. I have had to deal with many despairing sinners who would pull me down if I did not lift them up. I try to speak very good words for Christ when I meet with these dejected ones. I hear one say, "How far can Christ be life to a sinner? I feel myself to be utterly wrong. I am completely wrong. There is nothing right about me. Although I have eyes, I cannot see. Although I have ears, I do not hear. If I have a hand, I cannot use it. If I have a foot, I cannot run with it. I seem completely wrong."

Yes, but if you believe in Christ, even if you were still more wrong – that is to say, even though you were dead, which is the worst state in which a person's body can be – even though you were dead, yet you will live. You look at the spiritual thermometer and you ask, "How low will the grace of God go? Will it descend to summer heat? Will it touch the freezing point? Will it go to zero?" Yes, it will go below the lowest conceivable point – lower than any instrument can indicate. It will go below the zero of spiritual death. Even if you are not only wrong, but dead in your heart, if you believe in Jesus, you will yet live.

Someone else says, "I feel so weak. I cannot understand. I cannot comprehend these things. I cannot pray. I cannot do anything. All I can do is to feebly trust in Jesus." All right! Even if you had gone further than that, and were so weak as to be dead, you would yet live. Even if the weakness had turned to a dire paralysis that left you completely without strength, yet it is written, *He who believes in Me will live even if he dies.*

"Oh, sir," someone says, "I am so unfeeling." These people are generally the most feeling people in the world. "I am sorry every day because I cannot be sorry for my sin." That is the way they talk; it is very absurd, but it is still very real to them. "Oh," one says, "the earth shook, the sun was darkened, the rocks rent, and the very dead came out of their graves at the death of Christ, yet I remain unmoved."

> Of feeling all things show some sign,
> But this unfeeling heart of mine.[10]

Yet if you believe, as unfeeling as you are, you live; for if you were gone further than numbness to deadness, yet if you believe in Him, you will live.

Another person sighs, "Sir, it is not just that I have no feeling, but I am become objectionable and obnoxious to everybody. I am a weariness to myself and to others. I am sure that when I tell you my troubles, you would wish that I were at Jericho or somewhere else far away." I admit that such a thought has occurred to me sometimes when I have been very busy and some poor soul has grown tedious with rehearsing his seven-times-repeated miseries, but if you were to get more dull still, if you were to become so bad that people would rather see a corpse than to see you, yet remember that Jesus says, *He who believes in Me will live even if he dies.* Yes, if you went so far as to go in and out among people like a nervous ghost so that everybody got out of your way, it would not put you beyond the promise: *He who believes in Me will live even if he dies.*

"Oh, sir, I have no hope. My case is quite hopeless!" Okay, but even if you had got beyond that so that you were dead and did not even know you had no hope, yet if you believed in Him, you would live.

"Oh, but I have tried everything, and there is nothing more for me to try. I have read books, I have spoken to Christians, and I am no better off." No doubt it is quite so, but even if you had passed beyond that

---

10   This is from Joseph Hart's hymn "The Stubborn Heart" or "The Stony Heart."

stage so that you could not try anything more, yet if you did believe in Jesus, you would live.

Oh, the blessed power of faith – or rather, the matchless power of Him who is the resurrection and the life; for even if the poor believer were dead, yet shall he live! Glory be to the Lord who works so wonderfully!

To conclude, once you believe in Christ and receive new life, there is this sweet reflection for you: *Whosoever liveth and believeth in me shall never die.* Here is a very literal translation: *Every one who lives and believes on Me, in no wise shall die forever.* This is from the Englishman's Greek New Testament, and this could not be said any better. The believer may pass through the natural change called death, as far as his body is concerned, but his soul cannot die. Jesus says that He gives His sheep eternal life: *I give eternal life to them, and they will never perish; and no one will snatch them out of My hand* (John 10:28). *He who believes in the Son has eternal life* (John 3:36). *The water that I will give him will become in him a well of water springing up to eternal life* (John 4:14). *He who has believed and has been baptized shall be saved* (Mark 16:16).

Someone else says, "You don't know what I am." No, and I don't want to know what you are; but if you are so far gone that there seems to be not even a ghost of a shade of a shadow of a hope anywhere about you, yet if you now believe in Jesus, you will live. Trust the Lord Jesus Christ, for He is worthy to be trusted. Throw yourself upon Him, and He will carry you in His arms. Cast your whole weight upon His atonement; it will bear the strain. Hang on Him as the picture hangs on the nail, and seek no other support. Just as you are now, depend upon Christ with all your might, and as the Lord lives, you will live. As Christ reigns in you, you will reign over sin. As Christ comes to glory, you will partake of that glory forever and ever. Amen.

## Chapter 5

# The Believer Catechized

*Do you believe this?* (John 11:26)

The Savior said to Martha, *I am the resurrection and the life; he who believes in Me will live even if he dies, and everyone who lives and believes in Me will never die. Do you believe this?* (John 11:25-26).

When believers are full of sorrow, they can be assured that comfort is prepared that precisely fits their situation. For every lock that God has made, He has provided a key. Just as every blade of grass has its own drop of dew, so every grief has its comfort. I do not doubt that for every pain that grieves this mortal body, there is a relief among the herbs of the field, and for every disease there is a remedy in God's wondrous laboratory, if we could only find it. As for us who believe in the Lord Jesus Christ, we can rest assured that if we are weighed down by excessive sorrow, it is almost always our own fault, and it arises from a defect in our faith. If our faith were as strong as it should be, we would be *well content with weaknesses, with insults, with distresses, with persecutions, with difficulties, for Christ's sake* (2 Corinthians 12:10). We would find that as our tribulations abounded, our consolations would also abound through Christ Jesus.

It would be good, therefore, when we are greatly distressed, not to look so much to the apparent cause of the present trouble as to the condition of our own hearts. It would be wise to inquire about where our faith is lacking and what keeps us from laying hold upon the comfort provided for the present distress. Our faith is often defective because of lack of knowledge. A person cannot believe what he does not know.

My dear, tried friend, there is a promise in the Scriptures that would exactly meet your circumstance, and if grasped by faith it would immediately comfort you; yet it does not help you at all because you may never yet have read it, or having read it, you may never have paused over it and considered its meaning, and so you are needlessly distressed. Your relief lies close at hand, and is easy to apply.

Maybe you have not yet learned the whole wealth of gospel doctrines, and this also deprives you of comfort. You have laid hold upon the vital and saving part of revelation, but you do not know the strengthening and invigorating part of it. You have fed on the necessary bread of Christ's house, but not upon the delicious fruits of His garden. You have been in the field, but you have not walked in the garden to eat His pleasant fruits. Faith cannot believe what it does not know, and therefore you have missed *choice pieces with marrow, and refined, aged wine*, which could have been your strength and your joy (Isaiah 25:6).

We would all grow in comfort if we grew in grace and in the knowledge of our Lord and Savior Jesus Christ, and if we had a more intelligent appreciation of the preciousness of the truths that He has revealed. Faith can be defective through ignorance, and it can also be defective through a lack of appreciation of the person of Christ. It was this way in Martha's case. She did not know enough about her Lord to understand His power to meet her sorrow. The apostle Peter says, in the passage that I just quoted, *Grow in the grace and knowledge of our Lord and Savior Jesus Christ* (2 Peter 3:18), as if the knowledge of Jesus were indeed the most important and gracious knowledge that a believer can obtain, and so it is. If we are only half instructed about our Lord, we will only be half comforted. O mourners, you have not rated the Savior highly enough. You do not yet have a large enough idea of His love for you and of His design of infinite wisdom in permitting you to be afflicted.

If we knew the Lord Jesus better, our afflictions would be lightened and our hearts would even rejoice in them. If we only know You well, O blessed Christ, then if the same trials remained with us they would lose their gloom beneath Your smile, and we would even come to rejoice in them as ministering to our fellowship with You in Your sufferings. If we know Jesus well, sorrow loses its sting; surely even the bitterness of death is past.

It is not to be supposed that every true believer in Christ is definitely a perfect believer. Martha truly believed in Jesus, but she did not perfectly believe in Him. I do not know how many people reading this have, or rather, think they have, perfect faith. Such good people will get very little from this section of the book; but then, happily, they do not need it.

Those of us who have an imperfect faith – and I suspect that this would describe most of us –can gather instruction from the Savior's question to Martha: *Do you believe this?* (John 11:26). May the Holy Spirit cause it to be so. Let us imagine that we hear His loving lips asking us now about this truth and all of God's Word, *Do you believe this?*

We want to believe everything that is true, and we want to receive into our minds every doctrine that the Holy Spirit has revealed, for we want to perfect our discipleship. One of the privileges of a Christian is that *when He, the Spirit of truth, comes, He will guide you into all the truth* (John 16:13). We desire to believe everything that is within the range of our spiritual knowledge so that our faith, taking the entire range of divine truth, will be complete for every emergency and mighty in every conflict. Submit, then, to a heart-searching inquiry as to your faith, and hear Jesus ask by His Spirit, *Do you believe this?*

### Do You Believe This Particular Doctrine?

I will not now suggest any one doctrine above another, but will simply advise you to ask the question about every revealed truth: Do you believe this specific doctrine? You who are believers have faith in the Scriptures in general. You can boldly declare that you believe all that is written in the inspired volume from the first word of Genesis to the last word of the Revelation. The point now is to take each separate item out of this general mass of things believed, or supposed to be believed, look it over in detail, and then say with your heart and conscience, "I believe this."

It is easy to talk in general, and it is very easy to think that we have a large amount of faith, yet we may actually not have much faith, or none worth having. We might have put the treasure of truth into a bag that is full of holes, and so may have lost it as quickly as we have found it. We might think that we embrace the entirety of revealed truth, yet when we come to a quiet examination of our soul, we might find that much is slipping away from us by a process of questioning and doubt that we hardly want to admit.

Things believed and never used are like a sluggard's farm that lies uncultivated and is never tilled. We hardly call such land a farm, and can we call such belief real faith? Some truths taught in the Word of God are not even known by many who claim to be Christians, and we cannot believe what we do not know. It is the same situation as that suggested in the apostle's question, *How will they believe in Him whom they have not heard?* (Romans 10:14). If we do not see the surface meaning that is within our reach, we cannot be said to believe in any real sense.

When our Savior questioned Martha, she had already expressed her faith in certain great truths. She said, *Lord, if You had been here, my brother would not have died* (John 11:21). She believed in the Savior's power to heal the sick. She believed that as long as her brother still breathed, the power of Christ could have kept him alive. She was convinced that Jesus had power over disease and could restore the suffering to health. This was something worthy of her faith, but it was not enough. Our Lord set a further fact before her when He asked, *Do you believe this?* It is our duty to grow in knowledge and to exercise faith in proportion as we do so.

Next, Martha believed that although her brother was dead, the power of Christ's prayer was so great that He could do something, although she does not quite say what, to comfort the bereaved: *Even now I know that whatever You ask of God, God will give You* (John 11:22). She had faith in our Lord's influence with God in prayer, and that to an unlimited degree. She believed in Jesus as a mighty intercessor. She knew that He only had to speak with the Most High, and His request would certainly be answered. This is a very commendable amount of faith. I wish we all had that much faith. To have such faith was certainly admirable, but it was not enough to give her present comfort. Therefore, Jesus put before her a fact that was even more honorable to Himself, and then He added, *Do you believe this?*

Martha also expressed her firm conviction as to the certainty of the general resurrection: *I know that he will rise again in the resurrection on the last day* (John 11:24). She had learned this, no doubt, from the Old Testament Scriptures and from the general belief among orthodox Hebrews. She may also have learned this great truth from the teaching of the Savior Himself. She was a thoroughly sound believer in this great fundamental doctrine, but she had not yet seen the resurrection in the Christian light, and she had not yet understood our Lord's connection with it. She had not yet learned enough to give her comfort under her heavy loss, for it is clear that she derived very little consolation from the fact of a distant and general resurrection. She needed resurrection and life to come closer to home and to become more of a present fact to her.

Our Savior pointed her to a truth concerning Himself that would answer that purpose. He said to her, *I am the resurrection and the life; he who believes in Me will live even if he dies, and everyone who lives and believes in Me will never die. Do you believe this?* (John 11:25-26). Here was a well of comfort from which she had never drunk, because, like Hagar in the wilderness, she had never seen the divine supply (Genesis 21:16-19). Christ pointed her to it and asked her if she would drink.

I wish, dear friends, that all of us who call ourselves Christians would go over the Bible every once in a while and review the great doctrines in order. We should consider each one of them, asking ourselves, *Do you believe this?* Take, for example, that great and earliest of doctrines, the election of grace. *Those whom He foreknew, He also predestined to become conformed to the image of His Son* (Romans 8:29). *Blessed be the God and Father of our Lord Jesus Christ, who has blessed us with every spiritual blessing in the heavenly places in Christ, just as He chose us in Him before the foundation of the world, that we would be holy and blameless before Him. In love He predestined us to adoption as sons through Jesus Christ to Himself, according to the kind intention of His will* (Ephesians 1:3-5). Pause over these texts, consider their evident meaning, and then ask yourself, *Do you believe this?*

Some believers in Christ do not attempt to accept this doctrine, but even call it horrible. Others speak of it as so mysterious and impractical that it is not to be preached in public. I would invite such people to honestly look the doctrine in the face and see whether they believe it or not. If they do not, they might as well take a pen and cross out all passages of the Word of God that plainly teach it. They would not want to do this, and yet they do that which amounts to the same thing. When a person is afraid of or ashamed of a doctrine, he has serious cause to suspect that he does not believe it.

Take another grand truth: *A man is justified by faith apart from works of the Law* (Romans 3:28). *Having been justified by faith, we have peace with God through our Lord Jesus Christ* (Romans 5:1). *He that believeth on him is not condemned* (John 3:18 KJV). The perfect pardon of the believer, the complete justifying power of the righteousness of Christ to them that believe, is plainly taught in the Bible. *Do you believe this?* If you do, why do you call yourself a miserable sinner every day when you are not so any longer, but are a blood-washed saint and a happy child of God? Why do you talk about your sin as if it were not forgiven, and why do you speak of yourself as if you were still *children of wrath, even as the rest* (Ephesians 2:3), when you are justified in Christ Jesus and accepted in the Beloved? Look at the scriptural truth and at your conduct, and then ask yourself, *Do you believe this?*

Suppose you turn to the Scriptures and read of the union of Christ with His people. *I in them and You in Me, that they may be perfected in unity* (John 17:23). *I am the vine, you are the branches* (John 15:5). When you read this, ask yourself, *Do you believe this?* Do you believe that all who live unto God are one with Christ? *Do you believe this?* If so, why are you troubled as to your acceptance with God since you are one with Christ? Why do you think that you will ultimately perish if you are one with Him? Will Christ lose the members of His body? Do you think that one after another of the limbs of His spiritual body will rot away and die? Has He not said, *Because I live, you will live also* (John 14:19)? *Do you believe this?*

Maybe people will say of a certain truth that it is a difficult or a mysterious doctrine, or one that seems almost too good to be true; but this is missing the mark. The one question is, Is it given to us by God in His Word? Paul asked, *King Agrippa, do you believe the Prophets? I know that you do* (Acts 26:27). So I would ask you, if you believe the prophets and the apostles, why do you not believe each of those great truths that God has spoken by them? And if you believe that these truths have been revealed to us by God in His Word, how dare you cast a slur upon them by saying they are too difficult or complicated or mysterious, or something else!

I will not ask you to believe my statement or the statements of theologians and pastors, but turn to the infallible Book itself. See what is there written, and then ask yourself, *Do you believe this?* As you come across this statement or that statement of the Holy Scriptures, do not dismiss it, object to it, twist it, or try to see if some scholar has tried to explain the life out of it, but believe it just as you find it. If you cannot do so, stop until you can. Cry out to God for further light until you can answer the Savior's question without hesitation, saying with Martha, *Yes, Lord* (John 11:27).

*Do you believe this?* This question, well-managed and pressed home, will enlarge the range of faith! It will strengthen its grasp upon your heart and life! How rich our souls would become! Our inward confidence would feed upon wonderful food if we would simply treasure up each crumb of revealed truth. Search the Scriptures and take the teaching of the Word of God in detail, line by line and word by word, and say to your soul, *Do you believe this?* Ask for an anointing from the Holy One that you *may be able to comprehend with all the saints what is the breadth and length and height and depth, and to know the love of Christ which surpasses knowledge* (Ephesians 3:18-19). You will benefit much from this first point if you will conscientiously and consistently ask yourself, *Do you believe this?*

**Do You Believe this Distinct Doctrine?**
I find, especially among members of certain churches, great cloudiness regarding their faith. I would not judge severely, but I notice that those converted people who come to us from certain groups, which I will not now name, believe the gospel, but it is too much after the manner of the coal miner in the old story. He was asked, "What do you believe?"

He answered, "I believe as the Church believes."

He was then asked, "But what does the Church believe?"

He replied, "The Church believes what I believe."

He was further asked, "And what do you and the Church believe?"

He answered, "We both believe the same thing."

There was no getting any further with him. Is not this kind of faith common enough at this day? Many who are called Christians have this blind faith and little more. This weak faith in you know not what is more proper for fools than for rational beings. Let those delight in it who are of a low mind or who are too lazy to think for themselves. As for us, as long as we have eyes, we will not give in to walk blindfolded. We like people to do their own thinking. Hang your clothes out to dry, if you want to, but you should do your thinking at home. You will not reach the land of truth unless you will pay your way there by thinking about the teaching of the Lord.

You can believe or not believe whatever I tell you, but I plead with you not to accept it for any other reason than that, in your own judgment, it is in accordance with the mind of God as unveiled in Holy Scripture. God has given each person a judgment, a conscience, and understanding, and the owner of them is obligated to use them. Light is not given to everyone in the same way, and so those who do not have great knowledge often use guides to help them learn. However, light can only be seen by a person's own eyes, and he cannot see objects by someone else looking at them for him.

By experience, some people have learned much more than others, and so they are useful helpers, but no one's experience of grace can take the place of my own. We each must feel and know the divine life in our own soul. Just as all food must be chewed and digested by each person for the nourishment of his own body, so must truth be read, observed, learned, and inwardly digested by each person for the nourishment of his own soul. The Church of Rome says to yield an implicit faith to their Church. This is a fine plan for their priestly system, and you see through the scheme in a minute; but we say the very reverse, telling you not to believe a single word that any of us, or all of us put together, say to you if it is contrary to the Word of God.

Read the Word of God for yourselves. Search the Scriptures and see whether these things are so or not, just like the Bereans of old did (Acts 17:11). They were called noble because of it, and you will be noble if you rise to the dignity of your strength. With the help of God, use your own sense and understanding, and pray for the teaching of His Spirit so that you can know what the truth is.

Our Savior put a specific truth before good Martha in clear terms.

He left the general haze of the resurrection in which she believed, and He said, "I who stand before you am the resurrection and the life. *Do you believe this?*" Do you believe the doctrine put in this clear form and shape? He gave her crisp, sharp, definite teaching, and asked, *Do you believe this?* He did not set before her a vague, unclear, shadowy image of truth, but He presented to her a solid, substantial statement that He Himself was the resurrection and the life, raising those who believe in Him from the dead, and keeping in life those who, being alive, believe in Him. Then He demanded, *Do you believe this?*

A great many people see doctrines in a kind of dim, hazy light, and in that low light they exercise a sort of faith, but they will never get comfort out of truth in that way. We must believe revealed truth as we see it, in its own clear, well-defined, and accurate form as Scripture shows it. For instance, the doctrine of the atonement is robbed of half its delight if it is not clearly stated. Thousands of Christians believe in a kind of atonement, a means of reconciliation, a sort of propitiation made by Christ that in some way or another brings us to God; but, beloved, you need to believe that *He Himself bore our sins in His body on the cross* (1 Peter 2:24), and that *the* Lord *has caused the iniquity of us all to fall on Him* (Isaiah 53:6). *Do you believe this?*

*He made Him who knew no sin to be sin on our behalf, so that we might become the righteousness of God in Him* (2 Corinthians 5:21). *Do you believe this?* Read the fifty-third chapter of Isaiah, in which you have substitution set forth most clearly. Yes, read the chapter through and pause over the different verses, such as verse eleven: *As a result of the anguish of His soul, He will see it and be satisfied; by His knowledge the Righteous One, My Servant, will justify the many, as He will bear their iniquities.* Then ask yourself, *Do you believe this?*

The very life, soul, and sweetness of atonement will be found in the substitution of the innocent Savior for the guilty sinner in actually bearing the penalty of sin, the real payment of the debt. It is then that I know I am clear, because He, in my place, has vindicated justice, honored the law, and glorified God. *Do you believe this?*

Dear friend, ask God to give you grace so that you can believe in what Christ has taught and in what the prophets and the apostles have spoken, exactly as it was meant for you to believe – not in a haphazard, unreal way, but with your whole heart, soul, and mind, accepting God's Word as it stands, in all its clearly cut lines and features. Have a quick and true answer to the question, Do you believe this distinct and clear truth? Answer, *Yes, Lord.*

### Do You Believe This Difficult Truth?

Certain truths are hard to grasp. There are points about them that almost stagger faith until faith rises to its true character and is no longer reduced to carnal reasoning; but these difficult things should still be believed. It was not easy for Martha to understand how the Lord Jesus could Himself be the resurrection and the life, and yet her brother was dead. It was not an easy truth for her to believe, and it is not easy for us. How can He who died be life? How can He whose members are still in the grave be the resurrection? How can the Son of Man have such wonderful power that resurrection and life should be entirely dependent upon Him? How can these things be? We know the fact, but we do not understand it. It is good for us if we do not think that we need to understand it, but regard it as sufficient for us to believe what is revealed, even though it may seem like a bottomless pit to our reason.

Indeed, it was hard for Martha to believe that her Lord was the life, because it seemed contrary to her experience. *He who believes in Me will live even if he dies* (John 11:25). She might hope that this was possible in the case of Lazarus, but then the Lord said, *Everyone who lives and believes in Me will never die* (John 11:26). How could that be true? Lazarus lived and believed in Jesus, and yet he had died. Martha's experience seemed to be contrary to Christ's statement, and this might have made it difficult to believe; therefore the Lord asked, *Do you believe this?*

But, my brethren, when we become Christians, we no longer consider difficulties of belief, for we take the Scriptures upon divine authority and submit ourselves implicitly to their teaching. At any rate, I have done so. What the Catholic Church is to the Roman Catholics, the Bible and the Holy Spirit are to me. Believing the Bible this way, no difficulty remains that is even half as great as those that I have overcome.

I believed, first of all, that God was in Christ, that He who made the heavens and the earth came down below and took upon Himself human nature, was born in Bethlehem, was cradled in a manger, and was nourished by his mother. After having believed that, I can believe anything. Once belief in the incarnate God is accepted, no difficulty needs to stagger my faith. Martha's speech, *I have believed that You are the Christ, the Son of God, even He who comes into the world* (John 11:27), proved her readiness to believe everything else that Jesus might teach.

To begin with, the incarnation (which no one can be a Christian without believing) is so profound a mystery that other teachings are simple in its presence. *Without controversy great is the mystery of godliness: God was manifest in the flesh* (1 Timothy 3:16 KJV). Once you rejoice in the light of this, which is the very daystar of hope to us – that God has taken our human nature into union with Himself – you are ready for all light. Just let me know that God says anything is true, and that is enough for me.

I do not quite join with the poor old woman in her words, but I agree with her spirit, who put her unquestioning faith in Scripture in the most unguarded way. When someone ridiculed her for believing that the whale swallowed Jonah, she said, "Dear, if the Word of God said that Jonah swallowed the whale, I would believe it." Brethren, humble yourselves before the utterance of God. Not before man's decree or dogma, not before the utterance of priest, presbyter, pastor, or philosopher, but before God, who cannot err, we humble our souls. In Him you must place implicit faith. Whatever He says, we must believe it. This is not just how it should be in one case or even in twenty, but in everything that He says.

*Do you believe this?* Yes. *This*. Whatever it is. Yes. If it is indeed taught in the infallible Scripture by the Holy Spirit of God, we believe it. If your faith does not rise to this level, it will suffer for it. One day our Lord said to a group of His followers, *Unless you eat the flesh of the Son of Man and drink His blood, you have no life in yourselves. He who eats My flesh and drinks My blood has eternal life, and I will raise him up on the last day. For My flesh is true food, and My blood is true drink. He who eats My flesh and drinks My blood abides in Me, and I in him* (John 6:53-56).

What happened next? Read on. *Therefore many of His disciples, when they heard this said, "This is a difficult statement; who can listen to it?". . . As a result of this many of His disciples withdrew and were not walking with Him anymore* (John 6:60, 66). They asked, *How can this man give us His flesh to eat?* (John 6:52), and they came to the conclusion that it could not be; so they deserted their teacher.

Do we want to do this? The Lord Jesus Christ at the very beginning of His ministry prepares us to believe hard things. He tells us to count the cost about this, as well as about everything else. Although we already believe certain mysteries, there are many more that we do not know of as yet, which will in due course demand our faith. When Jesus told Nicodemus about being born again, and that had shaken him, Jesus said to him, *If I told you earthly things and you do not believe, how will you believe if I tell you heavenly things?* (John 3:12), as if even regeneration, which is really full of heavenliness, was only a common truth compared with what Nicodemus had yet to believe.

If Nicodemus had said, "Good Master, I can go as far as this, but I reserve my judgment and will go no further," then the ruler of the Jews and the Son of God would have parted, for he cannot be Christ's disciple who will not receive all Christ's words, no matter what those words may be. *Do you believe this?* Do you believe this difficult truth?

I ask this very earnestly to some of you because it may be that some of you are in trouble at this moment because of lack of faith in a promise or a doctrine that seems difficult to you. You have a promise: *When you walk through the fire, you will not be scorched, nor will the flame burn you* (Isaiah 43:2). *Do you believe this*, even though all things appear to be consumed in the heat of your affliction?

Maybe you are under a particular cloud and dense gloom. Jesus declares, *I am the Light of the world; he who follows Me will not walk in the darkness, but will have the Light of life* (John 8:12), and *I have come as Light into the world, so that everyone who believes in Me will not remain in darkness* (John 12:46). *Do you believe this?* Can you laugh at impossibility and say it will be done because God has said it? Do you not know that *things that are impossible with people are possible with God* (Luke 18:27)? Can your faith leap over the head of carnal reason? Can you wave current circumstances and the conclusions of your own judgment aside as you say, *Let God be found true, though every man be found a liar* (Romans 3:4)? If so, you have the faith that will comfort and bless you, but if not, like Martha, you will be bowed down with sorrow since you have not yet believed the truth that can comfort you.

**Do You Believe This Truth as It Stands Connected with Jesus?**
I called your attention just now to the fact that Martha believed that there would be a resurrection. "Yes," said Christ, "but I am the resurrection. *Do you believe this?*" It is one thing to believe doctrine, but it is another thing to believe that doctrine as it is embodied in the person of Jesus Christ. *Do you believe this?* The comfort lies in believing the truth as you find it in Him who is the truth.

Martha was first called upon to believe in Christ's personal power. "The dead will rise," said Martha. "True, Martha; but do you believe that I will make them rise, that it is through Me that the dead will live? Do you believe that I am the life and resurrection? *Do you believe this?*"

Martha was also to believe in His present power. Notice that. "Even now," Jesus said, *I am the resurrection and the life; he who believes in Me will live even if he dies, and everyone who lives and believes in Me will never die* (John 11:25-26). It is one thing to believe that Jesus will have power to raise the dead at the last day, but do we believe that He is *even now* the resurrection and the life? Oh, the joy of believing in the personal power of Christ and in the present power of Christ! Jesus, the I Am (John 8:58), says, *I am the resurrection and the life.*

Moreover, Martha was called on to believe in the union of Christ with His people. She was called on to believe that they are so one with Him that they are partakers of His life, that if they would come under the power of death they would be delivered out of it, and that being out of the power of death they will never come under it. In Christ the dead will live, and the living will not die.

"Oh," someone says, "but I do not understand this, for I see good people die." Yes, you see what you think is death, but they do not truly die. They rise into a higher life. That which is the essence of death never touches believers. They *depart out of this world to the Father* (John 13:1). They go to be with Christ, which is far better (Philippians 1:23), but they do not die. Death as a judicial sentence, in its innermost meaning, never comes near to those for whom Jesus has died upon the cross. His death, in their place, is the death of death to them. *Do you believe this?*

Ask yourself if you really believe that Christ Jesus has all power in heaven and in earth (Matthew 28:18). Ask yourself if you really worship Him as God over all, *blessed forever* (Romans 9:5). Do I really believe that He is able to do exceeding abundantly above all that I ask or even think (Ephesians 3:20)? When I come in prayer before God, do I also believe in Christ so that I remember His promise: *Whatever you ask in My name, that will I do* (John 14:13)? Christ Himself will give you all things.

Do you have such an idea of your Lord that you know that He can do all things for you now, and that in answer to your prayer He can grant you any blessing and save you out of any and every trouble? *Do you believe this?* If you do not, you do not have the right idea of Christ, for *He is Lord of all* (Acts 10:36). "Thou art the King of glory, O Christ,"[11] and as such we do believe in You, we trust You, and we find comfort in Your present, personal power!

### Do You Believe That This Truth Is Applicable to You Now?

That was the point with Martha, and this was where she fell short. She believed that everyone would rise. But Jesus basically said, "Do you believe that I am the resurrection and the life? If this is true, I am able to raise your brother at once. *Do you believe this?*" Notice that we sometimes accept great truths, yet are staggered by lesser truths. It may be that the great truth has no practical bearing upon us right now, while the present truth, although it is somewhat less in other respects, has a greater practical bearing upon us and our present situation. We doubt the promise that is most necessary to our comfort.

Martha believed that everyone would rise. Therefore, it was a much smaller thing to believe that one person would rise. She doubted whether Lazarus could rise because he was in the grave, yet she believed that millions upon millions would rise from the ground. Undoubtedly that was because of the distance of the time and the scene. She must have had some thoughts like that, for the general resurrection is the greater difficulty. Is it hard to believe that Lazarus can rise who has been dead

---

[11] This is likely a reference to George Frideric Handel's "Thou Art the King of Glory" from his *Dettingen de Deum*.

four days? Well, then, it is much harder to believe that bodies can be made alive that have been dead several hundred years.

Yet Martha did believe that the dead would rise at the resurrection at the last great day – not only those bodies that were stinking, but those whose bodies had been decayed by corruption and scattered by the four winds of heaven to the utmost ends of the earth. She believed the miracle on the grand scale. That is what she said, but when it came time to demonstrate her belief about only one person who had only been dead four days, she could not believe it.

Martha believed that there would be a general resurrection of all types of people, yet if that could be believed, it should have been much easier to expect that a favorite of Christ like Lazarus should rise. Jesus loved Lazarus. Certainly He would call him from the tomb. Martha professed to believe the larger truth, and then she staggered at the less, because it was applicable to her.

I ask you to see whether you are not often walking in the same path. Over there is a poor soul who believes that Jesus Christ can wash away all sin. Now, my dear friend, do you believe that He can wash your sin away? That is the point, because all the sins of millions are much greater than yours can be, and if Jesus can take away the sin of so many, He can certainly take away yours. *Do you believe this?* Will you come and trust Him for yourself?

And you, Christian, you believe in general that all things work together for good to those who love God (Romans 8:28). Do you believe that all your difficulties, small and great, are working good for you? Will that toothache of yours work for your good? Do you believe that yesterday's bad debt will work for good? Do you believe that the death of your child will work for good?

You know it must be easier to believe that the events of one day will work for good than to believe that all things in the world throughout life will do so, and yet it may be that you are dismayed at your present trials and you confess your misgivings. Do you have faith in everything except that which would comfort you? Do you have everything except the special requirement of the hour? How strange! How sad! The carpenter needs to drive a nail, and he has all his tools with him except his hammer! What is he to do? What is the good of all his other tools? If you can believe everything except the truth that would comfort you at this present moment, you are depriving yourself of comfort and strength.

Do you believe this present promise, given for this very day? The Lord has said that He will never leave you nor forsake you (Hebrews 13:5). *Do you believe this?*

> *Underneath are the everlasting arms* (Deuteronomy 33:27). *Do you believe this?*

> *Thy shoes shall be iron and brass, and as thy days, so shall thy strength be* (Deuteronomy 33:25 KJV). *Do you believe this?*

God's Word is as the tree of life that yields its fruit every month (Revelation 22:2). What a blessing to take the fruit from the tree of life in its month, just when it is ripest and fullest of flavor! God has said, *Delight yourself in the LORD; and He will give you the desires of your heart* (Psalm 37:4). Since you delight in Him, He will hear your prayer and will give you the light of His countenance (Psalm 4:6). *Do you believe this?*

## Do You Believe This Practical Truth?

Martha said that she believed it, but her actions did not prove it. She demonstrated her belief in the Lord's word in her declaration, *Yes, Lord; I have believed that You are the Christ, the Son of God, even He who comes into the world* (John 11:27). However, she did not believe so as to act on the belief. Samuel Taylor Coleridge said, "Truths, of all others, the most awful and mysterious, and at the same time of universal interest, are too often considered as so true, that they lose all the power of truth, and lie bed-ridden in the dormitory of the soul, side by side with the most despised and exploded errors."[12]

How true that is! Do you not know people who are better than their creed? Why is that? It is for the very same reason that many people are worse than their creed. It is because their creed is asleep and is not operating upon them. They believe as though they did not believe. This is a poor imitation of faith. I could tell you that there is a house on fire

---

12   This is from Coleridge's *Aids to Reflection*.

in your town at this moment. I could know it as a fact and could tell you of it, and you would believe it. But what do you care? None of you move. But if you saw the fire engine speeding down the street and you believed that your own house was on fire, then you would rush out to see. Your belief would come a little more home to you as your own concern.

In the same way, there are certain truths that do not seem to concern us much, at least for now. They are true and important, but they operate no more upon us than if they were fictitious. Martha said she believed in Jesus as the resurrection and the life, yet what was her action? Christ commanded the bystanders to take away the stone from the sepulcher, and she interposed with her cry, *Lord, by this time there will be a stench* (John 11:39). She feared the unpleasant consequences of uncovering such a body of corruption, even though He who is the resurrection and the life stood at the grave's mouth. Oh, Martha, where is your faith in Him?

Martha said that she believed in Jesus as the resurrection and the life, and yet she was afraid that her brother would not rise, even though the Mighty One stood there to raise him. Is she not just like you and me? We believe that God hears prayer, and therefore we pray; but if the Lord wants to surprise us, He only has to answer our requests. I have seen God's children running with vast astonishment to tell their friends, "How wonderful! Such a marvelous thing has happened to me! I prayed and God answered my prayer!" Is it an amazing thing that God would do as He said He would?

They put these things in books as marvels, and they title the book *Remarkable Answers to Prayer.* Is it remarkable that it is cold when it freezes? Do we speak of the remarkable warmth of the sun's beams in the middle of summer? Is it remarkable that the fires in our houses should warm us when we put our hands to them? Is He a remarkable God because He says He will hear prayer and does it? An answer to prayer should be remembered with gratitude, yet it should be regarded as the most natural thing in all the world that our heavenly Father would fulfil His promises to His children. It is a great wonder that God would promise, but it is not a wonder that He would do what He says He will do. It is marvelous that God would promise to hear prayer, but it is no wonder at all that He keeps His word when He has promised to do so.

Brethren, we are to a great degree impractical in other respects also, and we can take up many truths that we do not act upon and say to our heart, *Do you believe this?* A believer might say today, "I am so weak in spirit that I will utterly fall and perish in the end." I could respond, "Do you believe God?" The Lord has said, *He gives strength to the weary, and to him who lacks might He increases power* (Isaiah 40:29). *Do you believe this?*

I could go to another believer who is mourning and crying because of his poverty, and say to him, "God has said, *No good thing does He withhold from those who walk uprightly* [Psalm 84:11]. *Do you believe this?*" What would the complainer say? How could he reconcile his discomfort and his murmuring with his belief in the comforting promise?

My brethren, let us then go over these matters in our souls. We call ourselves believers, but are we believers at all? If we doubt the precious things of God one after another when they come before us in detail, where is our faith? Let us plead with God to grant us grace that we will put our finger on this doctrine, on that promise, and on the other assurance, and say of each one, "Lord, I believe this, and I believe this, and I believe this, for I believe whatever You say in Your Word, and I know that it will be done just as You have said."

May God bless you, beloved, and be always with you, for Christ's sake. Amen.

## Chapter 6

# The Master

*She went away and called Mary her sister, saying secretly, "The Teacher is here and is calling for you."* (John 11:28)

I suppose by Martha's whispering the word "the Teacher," or "the Master," in Mary's ear that it was the common name by which the sisters spoke of our Lord to one another when He was not there. Maybe it was His usual name among all the disciples, for Jesus said, *You call Me Teacher and Lord; and you are right, for so I am* (John 13:13). It often happens that for people whom we love, we have some special title by which we speak of them familiarly when we are in the circle of those who join in our esteem of them. Instead of always using their official titles or their actual names, there is a name that we have attached to them that is associated with happy occasions or reminds us of their endearing character traits, and therefore it is very sweet to us.

I suppose that most of the disciples called Jesus "The Master," many of them adding with it the word "Lord." Mary, I suppose, was especially apt to use that term, for it was her name for the Lord. I imagine that she called him "my Master." Of course, Martha could not say to Mary, "Your Master is come," for that would have been to cast suspicion on her own loyalty to Jesus. Maybe she was not in a frame of mind to say, "our Master," remembering that He was master of so many other people, too, and half hoping that He might be Master over death itself. She therefore said, *The Master.*

It was an emphatic title: *The Master is here.* It is very remarkable that minds of a kindred spirit to Mary have always loved this title of "the Master." That wondrous, sweet, mystic poet and dear lover of his Lord, George Herbert, whenever he heard the name of Jesus mentioned, would always say "my Master." He has given us that pleasing poem, "The Odor," which begins:

"How sweetly doth *My Master* sound! *My Master!*"

There must be something exceedingly precious about the title for a Mary and a Herbert to love that name above all other names. Jesus has many names, all full of music. This must be special indeed to be chosen above them all as the title that His most beloved followers prefer to give to Him. There are many among us who are ourselves accustomed to speak of the Lord as the Master, and although there are many other titles, such as "the Well-beloved," "the Good Shepherd," "the Friend," "the Bridegroom," "the Redeemer," and "the Savior," yet we still cherish a very special affection for this one name that gives forth to us "an oriental fragrancy," with which "all day we do perfume our mind."[13]

The word could just as well be translated "the Teacher," the authoritative teacher, for that is the gist of its meaning. I am glad to use the term "the Master," because usage and sweet association have made the word sacred to me, and also because we have still among us the custom of calling the head teacher in a school or college the Master. However, if the phrase is translated as "the Teacher is come," it might be closer to the actual meaning.

**I will say a few words now about the deep appropriateness of this title as applied to our Lord.**

Jesus is indeed the Master – the Teacher. What if I put the two together and say the Master-Teacher? He has a special suitableness for this office. To be a master-teacher, a person must have a masterly mind. Certainly all minds are not cast in the same mold and are not possessed with

---

13   These two phrases are also from George Herbert's poem "The Odor."

the same strength, depth, force, and quickness of action. Some minds are princely by their very formation. Even though they may belong to common people, the imperial stamp is on them. These minds cannot be smothered by a peasant's garment or kept down by the load of poverty. Master minds are recognized by an inherent superiority, and they force their way to the front.

I will not comment on the moral qualities of Napoleon, but a mind as vast as his could not have been hidden away forever among the soldiers in the ranks. He must become a captain and a conqueror. So, too, a Cromwell or a Washington must rise to be masters among men because the caliber of their minds was masterly. Such people see things quickly, and they hold them with a comprehensive grasp. They have a way of infusing faith into others about things that, before long, pushes them into a master's position with the common consent of everyone around them.

You cannot have someone with a little soul for a master-teacher. He may try to place himself into the chair of the teacher, but everyone will see that he is out of place, and no one will delight to think of him as his master. There are many painters, but there have been few Raphaels or Michaelangelos – few who could start schools to perpetuate their names. There have been many singers, but few have founded schools of tuneful thought in which they have been the beloved choirmasters. There have been many philosophers, but a Socrates or an Aristotle will not be found every day, for great teachers must have great minds, and these are rare among men.

The teacher of all teachers, the master of all the teachers, needs to be a grand, colossal spirit, head and shoulders above other men. Mary saw such a person in her Lord Jesus Christ, and we see such a one there also; Therefore, we use for our Lord the name of "the Master." In Christ Jesus we have divinity itself, with its omniscience and infallibility, and at the same time a complete manhood, harmonious in all its qualities, a perfect equilibrium of excellence in which there is no excess and no deficiency. You find in Him a perfect mind, and that mind is so human as to be intensely manly, yet also sweetly tender. In Jesus there was all the tenderness and sympathy of woman joined with all the strength and courage of man. His love was tender, but not effeminate. His heart was masculine, but not hard and stern. He was the complete man – unfallen manhood in its perfectness.

Our Lord was a man who made an impression upon all who came near Him. They either hated Him intensely or loved Him fervently. Wherever He was, He was seen to be a prince among the sons of men. The devil recognized Him and tempted Him beyond all others. Satan saw in Him a "foeman worthy of his steel,"[14] and took Him into the wilderness to have a duel with Him, hoping to defeat the race by conquering its clear leader. Even scribes and Pharisees, who despised everyone who did not make the borders of their garments broad (Matthew 23:5), could not despise this man. They could hate Him, but their hate was the unconscious reverence that evil is forced to give to superlative goodness and greatness.

Jesus could not be ignored and overlooked. He was a force in every place, a power wherever He was. He is a master, yes – "the Master." There is a magnificence about His whole human nature so that He stands out above all other men, like some mighty Alpine peak that stands above the lesser hills and casts its shadow upon the valleys.

But to be a master teacher, a person must not only have a master mind, but he must also have a master knowledge of that which he has to teach, and it is best if that knowledge is acquired by experience rather than by instruction. This was the case with our Lord Jesus. He came to teach us the science of life, and in Him was life. He experienced life in all its phases, and He was *tempted in all things as we are, yet without sin* (Hebrews 4:15). The highest were not above Him, and He did not regard the lowest as beneath Him, but He condescended to their infirmities and sorrows.

There are no dreary valleys of desolation that His feet have not walked. There are no lofty peaks of joy that He has not scaled. Wondrous was the joy as well as the sorrow of our Lord Jesus Christ. He leads His people through the wilderness, and like Hobab of old (Numbers 10:29-31), He knows where they should encamp in the wilderness, and He understands the way that they must travel to reach the promised land. He was made perfect through suffering (Hebrews 2:10).

He does not teach any truth as mere theory, but He knows truth as

---

14   "The Disclosure," a poem by Sir Walter Scott, tells of "the stern joy which warriors feel in foemen worthy of their steel."

a matter of His actual experience. He has tested the remedy He gives to us. If there is bitterness for us, He has consumed full bowls of it. If there is sweetness in His cup, He gives us of His joy. By personal acquaintance and experience, He understands very well all things that have to do with this life and godliness – and the whole realm of salvation from the gates of hell up to the throne of God. There is not a single chapter of the book of God's revelation or a single page of the book of experience that He does not understand. Therefore, He is fit to teach, having both a master mind and a master knowledge of that which He comes to impart.

Moreover, our great Master had a masterful way of teaching while He was here below. This is essential, for not everyone with vast knowledge and a great mind can teach others. Ability to teach is required. We know some whose words never seem to be in the language of ordinary people. If they have anything to say, they say it in a language of their own, which they and a few of their disciples probably understand, but it is unintelligible to ordinary people. Blessed is that teacher who teaches what he understands himself in a way that enables others to understand him.

I like the style of old William Cobbett when he said, "I not only speak so that people can understand me, but so that they cannot misunderstand me." That was the kind of teacher that Christ was to His own disciples. When they sat at His feet, He made truth so clear that the simplest people, even if uneducated, understood His message. By plain parables and phrases that caught the ear and won the heart, He brought down heavenly truths to ordinary minds as the Spirit of God cleansed those minds and made them able to receive the truth.

Not only did Jesus teach plainly, but He also taught lovingly. So gently did He explain things to His own disciples that it must have been a pleasure to be ignorant in order to require to be taught, and it must have been an even greater pleasure to continue to learn in such a way. The way in which He taught was as sweet as the truth that He taught. All who entered Christ's school felt at home, were pleased with their Master, and were confident that if they could learn anywhere, they would learn at His feet.

In connection with His teaching, the Master gave a measure of the

Holy Spirit – not the full measure, for that was reserved until He had ascended up on high and the Spirit would baptize the church; but He gave to each of His people a measure of the Spirit of God by which truths were not taught only to their ears, but also to their hearts. Oh, my brethren, we are not such teachers as Christ, for when we have done our best, we can only reach the ear. We cannot give the Holy Spirit, but He can. When the Spirit comes from Christ and takes of His things and reveals them unto us, then we see more of our Lord's masterly methods of teaching.

We can learn how much of a master Jesus is. He writes His lessons, not on the blackboard, *but on tablets of human hearts* (2 Corinthians 3:3). He does not just give us schoolbooks, but He is the book. He not only sets lessons before us, but He is the lesson. He demonstrates for us that which He wants us to do, so that when we know Him, we know what He has to teach, and when we imitate Him, we have followed the instructions that He gives.

Our Lord's way of incorporating His instruction in Himself is a truly magnificent way, and none can rival Him in it. Do not children learn infinitely more by example than they ever do by words? This is how our Master teaches us. *Never has a man spoken the way this man speaks* (John 7:46) is a great Christian proverb, but it might be surpassed by another one: "Never has a man acted the way this man acts," for this man's deeds and words complement each other. The deeds embody and enforce the words, give them life, and help us to understand them. Jesus is a prophet like Moses (Deuteronomy 18:15) because He is mighty both in word and in deed (Luke 24:19; Acts 7:22), and so He is the master of both prophets and teachers. His is a master mind, a master experience, and a master method of teaching. He is certainly rightly called *the Master*.

In addition to these things, dear friends, there was a master influence that Jesus, as a teacher, had over those who came within His range. They did not merely see, but they felt. They did not only know, but they loved. They did not just value the lesson, but they worshipped the teacher. What a master Christ was, whose very self became the power by which sin was restrained and ultimately cast out! It was by Christ Jesus that virtue was implanted and the new life was begun, nourished, and brought to perfection.

To have someone teach you who is very dear to you makes the lessons easy. No child learns better than from a mother qualified to teach, who knows how to make her lessons sweet by crystallizing them in the sugar of her own affection. It is then a pleasure, as well as a duty, to learn. But no mother ever won her child's heart (and there have been tender and affectionate mothers, too) as thoroughly as Jesus won the heart of Mary; or, I may say, as Jesus has won your heart and mine, if your heart feels the same as my heart feels to my Lord.

We do not need any reasonings from Him to prove what He says, for instead of reason and argument He is truth Himself. His love is the logic that proves everything to us. With Him we hold no debate, for what He has done for us has answered every question we could raise. If He tells us what we do not understand, we believe it. We ask if we may understand it, and if He tells us no, we stay where we are and believe the mystery. We love Him so much that we are as glad not to know as to know, if that is His will. We believe His silence is as eloquent as His speech, and that which He conceals is as kindly intended as that which He reveals.

Because we love Him, He exerts such an influence over us that we immediately accept and cherish His teaching. The more we know Him, and the more His inexpressibly delightful influence dominates our nature, the more completely we submit our imagination, thought, reason, and everything to Him. People might call us fools for it, but we have learned at Jesus' feet that *the world through its wisdom did not come to know God* (1 Corinthians 1:21), and that except we are converted and become like little children, we *will not enter the kingdom of heaven* (Matthew 18:3), and therefore we are not concerned when the world thinks we are childish and naive. The world is growing more manly and more foolish, and we are growing more childlike and more wise. We believe that to grow downward into our Lord Jesus is the surest and truest kind of growth. It is only when we have grown all the way down to nothing, and even lower than that – until we are less than nothing – that we will be fully grown in the school of Jesus. It is only then that we will have a degree in true learning, knowing *the love of Christ which surpasses knowledge* (Ephesians 3:19).

We can very rightly call Him Master who has a masterly mind, a masterly experience, a masterly way of teaching, and exerts a masterly influence over His students so that they are forever bound heart and soul to Him and consider Christ Himself to be His own greatest lesson, as well as the greatest of all instructors.

Having proved that our beloved Lord is well entitled to the name, let me add that He is by office the one and only Master of the church. There is in the Christian church no authority for any doctrine except Christ's word. The inspired Book that He has left us, commanding us never to take a letter away from it or add a syllable to it (Revelation 22:18-19), that Book is our life manual, our authorized creed, and our settled standard of belief. I hear much said about various theology books and books of divinity, but my own impression is that there never was but one body of divinity, and there never will be but one, and that is Jesus Christ, *for in Him all the fullness of Deity dwells in bodily form* (Colossians 2:9). The true church's body of divinity is Christ.

Some churches refer to other standards, but we know no standard of theology but our Master. Jesus said, *I, if I am lifted up from the earth, will draw all men to Myself* (John 12:32). We feel no pull toward any other master. He is the standard. *To him shall be the obedience of the peoples* (Genesis 49:10).

We are not of those people who will go no further than Martin Luther. Thank God for Martin Luther! God forbid that we should say a disparaging word about him, but were we baptized unto Martin Luther? No, we were not (1 Corinthians 1:13). Some people can never budge an inch beyond John Calvin, whom I reverence first of all mere mortal men; but still, John Calvin is not our master, but only a more advanced pupil in the school of Christ. He teaches, and as far as he teaches as Christ taught, he is authoritative, but where Calvin goes apart from Jesus, he is no more to be followed than Voltaire himself.

There are brethren whose one reference for everything is to the words of John Wesley. "What would Mr. Wesley have said?" is an important question with them. We think it is a little matter what he would have said, or what he did say, for the guidance of Christians, now so many years after his departure. It is far better to inquire into what Jesus says in His Word. Wesley was one of the greatest men who ever lived, but he is not our master. We were not baptized in the name of John Wesley or John Calvin or Martin Luther. We have only one Master, and that is Christ (Matthew 23:10).

There have been times in England when the government has set out to decide the rules and practices of the church. The government says, "Do this," and the Church of England must do it, or, "Don't do that," and the Church must obey. The Church must take its meat like any dog from the hand that patronizes her, and her collar, made of whatever brass or leather Caesar chooses to ordain, bears this motto: *You are slaves of the one whom you obey* (Romans 6:16).

The poorest minister in the most despised of our churches, whose poverty is thought to make him abhorrent (but whose poverty is his glory if he bears it for Christ's sake), would scorn to have any spiritual act of his church submitted to the judgment of the state, and he would sooner die than be dictated to in the matter of divine worship. What has the church to do with the state?

Our Master and Lord has set up a kingdom that allows no other King but Himself. We cannot bow, and will not bow, before decrees of Congress or Parliament and politicians and kings in spiritual things. Christ's church has only one head, and that is Christ, and the doctrines that the church has to teach cannot be judged by a church court, or a bench of bishops, or a synod of ministers, or a presbytery, or a conference. The Lord Jesus Christ has taught us certain things, and if His teaching is contradicted, the contradiction is treason against His crown. Even if the whole church were assembled, and that church were the true one, if it would contradict the teaching of Christ, its decrees should mean no more to a Christian than the whistling of the wind upon the mountains, for Christ is Master, and none but Christ. If an apostle or an angel from heaven preaches any other doctrine than that of our Lord, let him be accursed (Galatians 1:8). I would to God that all Christians stood up for this. Then would,

> "Sects and names and parties fall,
>     and Jesus Christ be all in all."[15]

He is the only teacher and the only legislator in these matters. A church

---

15   This is from Charles Wesley's hymn "Christ, from Whom All Blessings Flow."

has a right to carry out Christ's laws, but it has no right to make a law. The ministers of Christ are bound to carry out the rules of Christ, and when they do so, what is bound on earth is bound in heaven (Matthew 18:18); but if they have acted upon any rules except those of this Book, their laws are only worthy of contempt. Be they what they may, they bind no Christian heart. The yoke Christ puts on us will be our joy to wear, but the yoke that church leaders thrust upon us will be our glory to trample on. *If the Son makes you free, you will be free indeed* (John 8:36). *Stand fast therefore in the liberty wherewith Christ hath made us free, and be not entangled again with the yoke of bondage* (Galatians 5:1 KJV).

*The Master.* That is the name Christ should receive throughout the whole church, and He should be regarded always, and on all occasions, and in reference to all spiritual subjects, as the last Court of Appeal, whose inspired word is

> "The Judge that ends the strife
>     where wit and reason fail."[16]

That is what I have to say about appropriateness of the title, *the Master*, for our Lord Jesus.

## Now let us consider the special recognition that Mary gave to Christ as the Master.

How did she give that recognition? She became His student. She sat reverently at His feet. Beloved, if He is our Master, let us do the same. Let us take every word of Jesus, weigh it, read it, observe it, learn it, feed on it, and inwardly digest it. I am afraid we do not read our Bibles as we should. We do not attach such importance as we should to every shade of expression that our Master uses.

I would like to see a picture of Mary sitting at the Master's feet. Great artists have painted the Virgin Mary so often that they would do well to do something different and sketch this Mary looking up with a deep, fixed gaze, drinking it all in and treasuring it all up – sometimes startled by a new thought and a fresh doctrine, and then inquisitively waiting

---

16   This is from the Isaac Watts' hymn "Laden with Guilt, and Full of Fears."

until her face beams with unspeakable delight as new light floods her heart. Her attentive discipleship proved how truly Jesus was her Master.

Notice, too, that Mary was not only His disciple, but she was a disciple of no one else. I do not know whether Gamaliel was popular then, but she did not sit at his feet. There was probably some Rabbi Ben Simon or some other famous scholar at the time, but Mary never spent an hour with him, for every moment she could set apart was joyously spent at the feet of a far dearer Rabbi. She sat quite close to the teacher, not wanting to miss even a word!

Maybe she was afraid that she might be slow of heart, and so she got as close to the preacher as others do who have a little deafness in their ears. In any case, her favorite place was close at His feet. That shows us that since we are always dull of hearing in our souls, it is good to get very close to Jesus when we are hearing Him, and it is good to commune while we listen. Mary did not change from Him to someone else for variety's sake. No, the Master, her Master, her only Master, was the Nazarene, whom others despised, but whom she called her Lord.

She was a willing scholar, for *Mary has chosen the good part*, Jesus said (Luke 10:42). Nobody sent her to sit at Jesus' feet. She was drawn to Jesus, and she could not help going to Him. She loved to be there. She was a willing and delighted listener. She was never so happy as when she had her choice, and that choice was always to learn of Him. Children at school always learn well if they want to learn. If they must be forced to go to school, they still learn, but they do not learn as much in comparison to those who eagerly go. When they want to go, and when they love the teacher, they learn quickly, and happy is the teacher who has a class of students who has chosen him to teach them.

Mary could well call Jesus *the Master*, for she made Him her sole attention, her loving and delighted focus. Notice that in choosing Christ for her Master, she perseveringly remained devoted to Him. Her choice was not taken away from her, and she did not give it up. Martha looked very irritated one day. How was she to watch the roast meat and the boiling pan at the same time? How could she be expected to prepare the table and to take care of the fire in the kitchen too? Why could not Mary come? Martha frowned, no doubt, but it did not matter. Mary remained sitting at the feet of Jesus.

Maybe she did not even notice Martha's face. I don't think she did, for the saints do not notice other faces when Christ's beauty is to be seen. There is something so absorbing about Him that He takes you entirely into Himself, captivating you. When He does draw someone to Himself, He not only draws the person to Himself, but He draws all of the person to Himself. So Mary sat there still, and she continued to listen. Those children who do not just study every once in a while, but those who are always learning, will learn as they stick to their books. Mary recognized the Lord Jesus Christ's master-teacher designation by giving to Him that persevering attention that such a Master-teacher had a right to claim.

She bent humbly to Him, for while she sat at His feet to be near Him, she sat there, too, out of deep humility of spirit. She felt that it was her highest honor to be sitting in the lowest place, for lowly was her mind. Those who think least of themselves will learn most of Christ. When a place at His feet seems to be too good for us, or if we are more than content with it, then His words will fall as the rain and drop as the dew. We will be as the tender herbs that drink in sweet refreshment, and our souls will grow.

Blessed are you, O Mary! And blessed is each one of you if you can call Christ your Master and prove it as she did. You will have the good part that will not be taken away from you (Luke 10:42).

**Now let us consider the special sweetness of the name to us.**
I have shown why the title of *the Master* was especially recognized by Mary, and now I want to show that it has a special sweetness for us also. I love that name: *the Master* – my Master or my Teacher. I love that name in my own soul, because it is as a teacher that Jesus Christ is my Savior.

The best illustration I can give you is that of one of those poor little boys in the street without father and mother, or with parents worse than none. The poor child is covered with filth and rags. He is well known to the policemen, and he has seen the inside of many jails. But a teacher in a Christian charitable organization has found him and instructed him, and now he is washed and clothed and happy. Now that poor boy does not know the sweetness of "my father" or "my mother." He does not recognize anything in those titles. Maybe he never knew his parents, or only knew such a form of them as to disgust him. But with what energy he says, "My teacher!"

These little children say, "My teacher" with quite as much affection as others speak of their mothers. Where there has been a great moral change brought about by the influence of a teacher, the name "my teacher" has much sweetness in it. Hear now the parable of the little boy and his teacher! I was that little child. Truly, I did not think of myself as poor and dirty, for I was foolish enough to think my rags were fine garments and that my filth was my beauty. I did not know what I was.

My Teacher saw me, though, and He knew how filthy and how ragged I was. He taught me to see myself as I was – and also to believe that He could wash me whiter than snow (Isaiah 1:18). He went even further and actually washed me until I was clean before the Lord. My Teacher showed me a wardrobe of snow-white linen garments, and He clothed me in them. My Teacher has taught me a thousand things and has given innumerable blessings to me. I owe my salvation entirely to my Teacher, my Master, my Lord.

Can you say the same? I know you can if you are indeed a disciple of Jesus. "My Teacher" means to you "my Savior," for He saved you by teaching you about your disease and your remedy, teaching you how wrong you were, and making you right by His teaching. The word "master" or "teacher" has a delightful meaning to us, for it is by His teaching that we are saved.

Let me tell you how I, as a preacher, love the name "my Master." I like to feel that what I said to those people on Sunday was not mine. I preached my Master, and I preached what my Master told me. Some find fault with the doctrine. I do not mind that, because it was not mine; it was my Master's. If I were a servant and went to the front door with a message, and the gentleman to whom I took it did not like the message, I would say, "Do not be angry with me, sir. I have told you my master's message to the best of my ability, and I am not responsible for it. It is my master's word, not mine."

When there are no souls converted, it is dreary work and one's heart is heavy, but it is comforting to go and tell your Master. When souls are converted and your heart is glad, it is a happy and a healthy thing to give all the glory to your Master. It would be an awkward thing to have to act on someone else's behalf without having any advice from or communication with that person. That would be a serious burden and responsibility. However, blessed be God, between every true minister and his Master there is open communication, and he never needs to do anything by himself.

He can imitate the disciples of John the Baptist, who, when they had taken up his mangled body, went and told Jesus (Matthew 14:12). That is the thing to do. There are difficulties in all churches, troubles in all families, and cares in all businesses, but it is good to have a Master to whom you can go as a servant, knowing that Jesus has the responsibility of the whole matter. We only have to do what He tells us. If we step beyond our Lord's commands, the responsibility rests on us and trouble begins; but if we follow our Lord, we cannot go astray.

*My Master.* Is this not a sweet name to say when you are troubled, dear friends? Maybe some of you are in trouble now. It removes fear when you find out that He who sent the trouble is the Teacher who teaches you by the trouble. The Master has a right to use whatever form of teaching He likes. In our schools, much is learned from the blackboard, and in Christ's school, much is learned from affliction.

You have heard the story often, but I will repeat it again, of the gardener who had preserved a very special rose with great care. One morning when he went into the garden, it was gone, and he scolded his fellow servants and felt very distressed – until someone said, " I saw the master coming through the garden this morning, and I believe he took the rose."

"Oh, then," the gardener said, "if the master took it, I am content."

Have you lost a dear child, or a wife, or a friend? It was He who took your flower. It belonged to Him. Would you want to keep back what Jesus wants? We are asked to pray sometimes for the lives of good people, and I think we can, but I have not always exercised faith while pleading, because it seemed to me that Christ pulled one way and I pulled the other. I said, "Father, let them be here," and Jesus said, *Father, I desire that they also, whom You have given Me, be with Me where I am* (John 17:24), and so I could not then pull very hard. If you know that Christ is pulling the other way, you give up quickly. You say, "Let the Father have it. The servant cannot oppose the Master." *It is the LORD; let*

*Him do what seems good to Him* (1 Samuel 3:18). *I have become mute, I do not open my mouth, because it is You who have done it* (Psalm 39:9).

Our Master learned that lesson Himself that He now teaches to us. That is a very remarkable statement: *I praise You, O Father, Lord of heaven and earth, that You have hidden these things from the wise and intelligent and have revealed them to infants. Yes, Father, for this way was well-pleasing in Your sight* (Luke 10:21). It pleased God to pass by the wise and prudent (Matthew 11:25), and therefore it pleased Christ that it should be so.

It is good to have our hearts like that poor shepherd to whom a gentleman said, "I wish you a good day."

He replied, "I never knew a bad day."

"How is that, my friend?"

"The days are just as God chooses to make them, and therefore they are all good."

"Well," said the other, "don't some days please you more than others?"

"No," he said. "What pleases God pleases me."

"Well, but do you not have a choice?" said the other.

"Yes, I have a choice, and my choice is that I choose that God would choose for me."

"But do you not have a preference whether you would live or die?"

"No," he answered, "for if I am here, Christ will be with me; and if I am in heaven, I will be with Him."

"But suppose you had to choose."

"I would ask God to choose for me," he said.

Oh, what a sweet simplicity that leaves everything with God. This is calling Jesus *Master* to perfection:

> Pleased with all the Lord provides,
> > Weaned from all the world besides.[17]

Once again, dear friends, it is sweet to us to call Jesus *Master*, because in so doing we take a position that is easy to reach, and yet is most delightful. To call Him our Bridegroom – what an honor it is to be so closely related to the Son of God! "Friend" is a familiar and honorable title.

---

17  This is from a Charles Wesley hymn that begins with "Lord, if Thou Thy grace impart."

To call him *Master*, though, is often easier, and it is quite as sweet. It is pure delight to us to be in His service, even if we take no higher place. If our hearts are right, to do whatever the Lord asks and commands is as much as we can ask for.

Though we are now sons and not slaves, and therefore our service is of a different character from what it ever was before, yet our service to Him is our delight. What will heaven be but perpetual service? Here we labor to enter into rest (Hebrews 4:11), but there they enter into rest while they labor. Rest is the perfect obedience of fully sanctified spirits. Do you not desire that? Will it not be one of your greatest joys in heaven to know that you are His servant? The glorified ones are called His servants in heaven. *His bond-servants will serve Him; they will see His face, and His name will be on their foreheads* (Revelation 22:3-4). Cause us to be free from sin, and we would be in heaven now; earth would be heaven to us.

I want you, dear brethren in Christ, to go away saying this sweet phrase under your tongue: *my Master, my Master.* You will never hear better music than that: *my Master, my Master.* Go and live as servants should live. Be sure that you truly make Him your Master, for He says, *If I am a master, where is My respect?* (Malachi 1:6). Speak well of Him, for servants should speak well of a good master, and no servant ever had so dear a Master as Jesus.

But there are some of you who cannot say this. I wish you could. Jesus is not your master. Who is, then? You have a master somewhere, for *you are slaves of the one whom you obey* (Romans 6:16). If you obey the lusts of the flesh, your master is your flesh, and the wages will be corruption, for the flesh comes to corruption, and nothing better. If your master is the devil, his wages are death. Run away from such a master. When servants leave their masters, they are usually required to give notice, but this is a case in which no notice should ever be given. When the prodigal son ran away from feeding the swine, he never stopped to give notice that he was going to leave the pigs, but started off immediately (Luke 15:20).

I recommend that every sinner run by the grace of God directly away from his sins. Staying to give notice is the ruin of many. They intend to be sober, but they must treat their good intention to another glass or two. They intend to think about divine things, but they must go to the theater once more. They are willing to serve Christ, but tomorrow – not tonight.

If I had such a master as you have who live in sin, I would get up at once and run away. I would say, by the grace of God, "I will have Christ for my Lord." Look at your grim master. Look at his cunning eyes! Can you not see that he is a flatterer? He intends your ruin. He will destroy you as he has destroyed countless others already. That horrid glance of sin, that enticing desire – consider them and abhor them. Do not serve a master who, though he gives you fair promises, labors for your destruction! Get up and run away, you slaves of sin!

Eternal Spirit, come and break their chains! Sweet star of liberty, guide them to the free country and let them find their freedom in Jesus Christ!

My Master rejoices to receive runaways. His door is open to vagrants and vagabonds, to the scum of the earth and the offscouring of all things, to people who are dissatisfied with themselves, and to miserable people who have no joy in their lives and are ready to lie down and die. *This man receives sinners* (Luke 15:2). He is like David, who went into Adullam, and *everyone who was in distress, and everyone who was in debt, and everyone who was discontented gathered to him; and he became captain over them* (1 Samuel 22:1-2).

Just as Romulus and Remus gathered the first population of new Rome by harboring escaped slaves and robbers whom they trained into citizens and made to be brave soldiers, so my Master has laid the foundation of the new Jerusalem, and He looks for the noblest of His citizens over there where sin and Satan hold them captive. He commands us to sound the silver trumpet and tell the slaves of sin that if they flee to Him, He will never give them up to their old master. He will set them free and will make them citizens of His great city, sharers of His abundance, and partakers in His triumphs. They will be His in the day when He makes up His jewels.

I remember preaching about this once, and an old sea captain told me after the sermon that he had served under the black flag of sin and Satan for fifty years, and by the grace of God he would tear down the old flag and run up the bloodred cross of Jesus Christ at the masthead.

I recommended to him not merely to change his flag, but to see that the vessel was repaired, but he wisely replied that repairing would be of no use to such an old water-logged hulk, and he had better scrap the old ship and get a new one.

I suppose that is the best thing to do – *to be dead to sin, but alive to God in Christ Jesus* (Romans 6:11). No matter what you do with the old wreck of fallen nature, you will never keep it afloat. The old man must be crucified with Christ (Romans 6:6). It must be dead, buried, and sunk fifty thousand fathoms deep, never to be heard of again. In the new vessel that Jesus launches in the day of our regeneration, with the blessed flag of atoning blood above us, we will sail to heaven escorted by irresistible grace, giving God the glory forever and ever. Amen.

## Chapter 7

# Jesus Wept

*Jesus wept.* (John 11:35)

A great storm was stirring in the mind of Jesus. We find, on looking at the original, that He was indignant and troubled. The margin of the Revised Version has a very literal translation, and instead of reading, *He was deeply moved in spirit and was troubled* (John 11:33), we find, "He was moved with indignation in the spirit, and troubled himself." What was this indignation? We cannot think that it was caused by the unbelief of His friends, or even by the pretended sympathy of those malicious Jews who wanted to accuse Him to the Pharisees, but we look further and deeper for the reason of this indignation.

Jesus now stood face-to-face with the last enemy, death. He saw what sin had done in destroying life, and even in corrupting the fine handiwork of God in the human body. He observed, also, the part that Satan had in all this, and His indignation was aroused. Yes, His whole nature was stirred. Some read it, "He roused Himself," instead of reading, as we have it in our version, "He was troubled." Certainly there seems to be an active sense in the expression. It was not so much that He was troubled as that "He troubled Himself." The waters of His soul were as clear as crystal, and therefore, when troubled, they were not muddied, but they were stirred up.

It could be seen that His holy nature was in a state of unrest, and an inarticulate expression of distress fell from Him. Between indignation at the powers of evil, grief for the family who had been bereaved by death, sorrow over those who stood by in unbelief, and a distressing realization of the effects of sin, the Lord's heart was evidently in a great storm. Instead of the thunder of threatening and the lightning of a curse, all that was perceptible of the inward tempest was a shower of tears – for *Jesus wept.*

A hurricane rushed through His spirit. All the forces of His soul were disturbed. He shuddered at the sight that was about to be set before Him. He was filled from head to foot with emotion, yet the result of the storm was not a word of terror or a glance of judgment, but simply a blessed shower of tears: *Jesus wept.* If all our righteous indignation displayed itself in tears of compassion, we would have fulfilled the text, *Be angry, and yet do not sin* (Ephesians 4:26).

*Jesus wept.* I have often felt annoyed with the man, whoever he was, who chopped up the New Testament into verses. He seems to have let the hatchet drop indiscriminately here and there, but I forgive him of much of his blundering for his wisdom in letting these two words make a verse by themselves: *Jesus wept.* This is a diamond of the first class, and it cannot have another gem set with it, for it is unique. It is the shortest of verses in words, but where is there a longer one in significance? Add even one word to the verse, and it would be out of place. No, let it stand in solitary sublimity and simplicity. You can even put a note of exclamation after it and let it stand in capital letters:

JESUS WEPT!

There is infinitely more in these two words than any preacher or student of the Word will ever be able to bring out of them, even though he would apply the microscope of the most attentive consideration. *Jesus wept.* This is an instructive fact. It is simple, yet amazing. It is full of consolation and worthy of our earnest attention.

*Lord, help us to discover for ourselves the wealth of meaning contained in these two words!*

We read about other men that they wept. Abraham, when he buried Sarah, wept (Genesis 23:2). Jacob had power with the angel, for he wept and prevailed (Hosea 12:4). We read often that David wept. His friend Jonathan and he once wept together, and were not less manly because of it, but were the more truly manly for weeping (1 Samuel 20:41). Of Hezekiah we read that he wept bitterly (2 Kings 20:3), and of Josiah that he poured forth tears over the sins of Judah (2 Chronicles 34:27). Jeremiah was a weeping prophet (Jeremiah 9:1). I could continue the list, but if I did, it would not be at all remarkable that the sons of a fallen father would weep.

With all the sin and sorrow that surrounds our lives, it is no marvel that it should be said of any man, "He wept." The earth brings forth thorns and thistles, and the heart brings forth sorrow and sighing. Is there a man or woman reading this who has not wept? Have we not all sometimes felt a sweet relief in tears? If I could look around at all of you, I could point to you one by one and say, "He wept, and he wept, and she wept, and she wept" – and no one would wonder that such has been the case. The marvel is that the sinless Son of God would, in the days of His flesh, know the meaning of strong crying and tears. The fact worthy to be noticed and recorded is that *Jesus wept*. We will meditate on that topic now, and may the Lord make our thoughts profitable!

First, I would remind you that *Jesus wept* because He was truly man. Secondly, *Jesus wept* because He was not ashamed of His human weakness, but allowed Himself to reveal the fact that He was, in this point also, *made like His brethren* (Hebrews 2:17). Thirdly, *Jesus wept*, and so He can teach us in this area. Fourthly, He is our comforter. Lastly, He is our example. We can only give a little space to each of these five things.

**First, *Jesus wept* because He is truly man.**
Many facts prove the completeness of the Lord taking up our nature. Not in a dream or in fiction was Jesus a man, but in reality and truth He became one of us. He was born of a woman, was wrapped in swaddling clothes, and was fed from His mother. He grew as a child, was obedient to His parents, and increased in stature and in wisdom (Luke 2:51-52). In manhood He worked, He walked, and He became weary. He ate as we do. We find it mentioned that He fasted and that He hungered. After His resurrection, He ate a piece of a broiled fish and of a honeycomb (Luke 24:42) to show that His body was real. His human nature was sustained, as ours is, by supplying it with food. Though on one occasion, sustained by divine power, He fasted forty days and forty nights, yet as

man He ordinarily needed food. He drank also, and He gave thanks both for food and drink (Mark 14:22-23; John 6:11).

We find Jesus sleeping with His head upon a pillow (Mark 4:38) and resting at the well of Sychar (John 4:6). He suffered all the innocent infirmities of our nature. He was hungry and disappointed when, early in the morning, He came to a fig tree seeking fruit, but found none (Matthew 21:18-19). He was weary: *Jesus, being wearied from His journey, was sitting thus by the well* (John 4:6). We know that He thirsted, for He said to the Samaritan woman, *Give me a drink* (John 4:7), and on the cross He cried in burning fever, *I am thirsty* (John 19:28). He was *made like His brethren in all things* (Hebrews 2:17). *He Himself took our infirmities and carried away our diseases* (Matthew 8:17). His humanity was our humanity to the full, although without sin. Sin is not essential to humanity, but it is a disease of nature. It is not a feature found in humanity as it came from the Creator's hand.

The Man of men, in whom all true humanity is found in perfection, is Christ Jesus. The fact that Jesus wept is a clear proof of this. He wept, for He had human friendships. Friendship is natural to man. That person is hardly a man who never had a friend to love. In going through the world, people make many acquaintances, but out of these they only have a few special objects of esteem whom they call friends. If they think they have many friends, they are probably misusing the name. All wise and good men have about them certain people with whom their conversation is more free and in whom their trust is more confident than in all others. Jesus delighted to find rest in the quiet home at Bethany, and we read that *Jesus loved Martha and her sister and Lazarus* (John 11:5). My brethren, every friendship opens a fresh door for grief, for friends are no more immortal than ourselves. *Jesus wept* at the grave of His friend just as you and I have done, and that we will likely do again. Behold your Lord weeping like David for his friend Jonathan, and see how human He is in His friendships.

*Jesus wept*, for He was truly human in His sympathies. He did not just walk around among us and look like a man, but He came into contact with us at a thousand points. Jesus was always in touch with sorrow. Happy are they who are in touch with Him! Our Lord saw Mary and Martha weeping, and the Jews weeping who were with her, and

He caught the contagion of their grief: *Jesus wept*. His sympathies were with those who were sorrowing, and for this reason, among others, He was Himself *a man of sorrows and acquainted with grief* (Isaiah 53:3).

He loved His Father in heaven first of all, and His Father's glory was His main object. However, He also intensely loved His chosen, and His sympathy with them knew no limit. *In all their affliction He was afflicted* (Isaiah 63:9). Jesus was far more tender toward humanity than any other man has ever been. He was the great Philanthropist. Man is often the cruelest foe of man. There is none more unkind to man than men. Not the elements in their fury, nor wild beasts in their rage, nor diseases in their terror have made such havoc among men as men drunk with the war spirit. When has there been such cruel hate on the part of the most savage monster toward man as that which has raged in the hearts of bloodthirsty warriors?

Our Lord was a perfect stranger to this hate. There was no hardness in His heart. He was love, and only love, and through His love He descended into the depths of grief with the beloved ones whose portion was sorrow. He carried out to the full that sacred precept, *Weep with those who weep* (Romans 12:15). Jesus was no unsuffering seraph. He was not a cherub incapable of grief, but He was bone of our bone and flesh of our flesh, and therefore, *Jesus wept*.

He was a man, dear friends, for He was stirred with human emotions. Every emotion that ever thrilled through your heart, as far as it is not sinful, had a similar emotion in the heart of the Lord Jesus Christ. He could be angry; we read in one place that He looked *around at them with anger* (Mark 3:5). He could be full of compassion; when was He not? He could be moved with compassion for a tired crowd, or moved with scorn toward a scheming ruler. Did He not speak with great indignation of the scribes and Pharisees? Yet was He not as tender as a nurse with a child when comforting the repentant?

He would not break the bruised reed or quench the smoking flax (Matthew 12:20), yet He uttered faithful warnings and clearly and forcefully exposed hypocrisy. Our Savior, at the moment described in our text, felt indignation, pity, love, desire, and other emotions. He who is full of tenderness was stirred from head to foot. He was troubled, and He troubled Himself. Just as when water is shaken in a small container, so His whole nature was shaken with a mighty emotion as He stood at the grave of Lazarus confronting death and him who had the power of it (Hebrews 2:14). Our Lord proved Himself a man when it was said that *Jesus wept*.

Note, too, that His pure body and sinless soul were originally made as ours are. When His body was formed according to that Scripture, *A body You have prepared for Me* (Hebrews 10:5), His body had in it the full ability of grief. He was made with the same ability to cry as we have. Where there is no sin, one would say there should be no sorrow, but in the formation of that blessed body, all the arrangements for the expression of grief were as fully prepared as in the case of any of us. His eyes were made to be fountains of tears, even as ours are. He also had about His soul all the capacity for mental grief.

As I said before, so I say again, that it would seem that there would be no tears where there are no transgressions – and yet the Savior's heart was made to hold sorrow, even as an amphora was made for wine. Even more, His heart was made pliant enough to be a reservoir in which great floods of grief could be gathered. See how the sorrow bursts forth in a mighty flood! Notice the record of that flood in these amazing words: *Jesus wept*.

Beloved, have a clear faith in the humanity of Him whom you rightly worship as your Lord and your God. Holding His divinity without doubt, hold His manhood without mistake. Realize the actual manhood of Jesus in all lights. Three times we read that He wept. Undoubtedly He often sorrowed when He was not seen, but He was seen weeping at least three times.

The instance in our text was the weeping of a Friend over the grave of a friend. A little further on, after a day of triumph, our Lord beheld the city and wept over it (Luke 19:41). That was the weeping of a Prophet concerning judgments that He foresaw. It is not recorded by any evangelist, but we are told in the epistle to the Hebrews that *with loud crying and tears*, He made appeal to Him who was able to save Him from death, and was heard in that He feared God (Hebrews 5:7). This third record sets forth the weeping of our Substitute, a sacrificial weeping, a pouring out of Himself as an offering before God.

Treasure up in your mind these three memories: the weeping of the Friend in sympathy with bereavement, the weeping of the Judge lamenting the sentence that He had to deliver, and the weeping of the Surety as He hurt for us, bearing griefs that were not His own, for sins in which He had no share. Thus, three times it was true that *Jesus wept*.

**Now let us see that *Jesus wept* because He was not ashamed of His human weakness.**
He could have forced back His tears; many men do so habitually. I do not doubt that there may be great sorrow, very great sorrow, where there is no open expression of it. In fact, most of you must have felt times when grief has struck you such a stunning blow that you could not weep. You could not recover yourself sufficiently to shed tears. Your heart was all on fire with anguish, but your eyes refused the cooling drops. If He had wanted to, the Savior could undoubtedly have hidden His grief, but He did not choose to do so, for he was never unnatural. As the holy child Jesus (Acts 4:27), He was free from pride, and He wore his heart where people could see it.

Remember His speech when He spoke to His disciples. He never hid His poverty. There is an idea held by some people that respectability is maintained by pretending to have more than enough, although you are really in great need. It is thought disreputable to seem to be poor, even when you are so. There may be something in the pretense, but our Lord did not pretend like that. He said, *The foxes have holes and the birds of the air have nests, but the Son of Man has nowhere to lay His head* (Matthew 8:20). *Though He was rich, yet for your sake He became poor* (2 Corinthians 8:9), and He was never ashamed to let it be known that He was poor.

Also, Jesus was *despised and forsaken of men* (Isaiah 53:3), and He did not pretend to be unaware of it. He did not try to pretend that He was exceedingly popular and that nobody had anything to say against Him, but He acknowledged that they had called the Master of the house Beelzebul (Matthew 10:25). He knew what they had called Him, and He was not ashamed of being made the target of ridicule and reproach. When they ascribed His miracles to the power of Satan, He met the charges with an overwhelming reply, but He was not ashamed that He was slandered or that He knew poverty.

As for His sufferings and death, how frequently do we find Him talking to His disciples about it, until Peter would have stopped Him if he could (Matthew 16:22)! Our Lord spoke of His being betrayed into the hands of sinners, being cruelly treated in hate, and spit upon (Matthew 17:22-23). He spoke openly of His being *lifted up* (John 12:32). He even dwelt upon His coming suffering and death. He had no wish to deny the fate that He knew awaited Him. Why not die and say nothing about it, if it must be so? Not so the Savior. He has become a man, and He is not bothered at that which necessarily follows as a part of His shame and suffering. Being found in appearance as a man (Philippians 2:8), He became obedient to all that was required of His manhood, and before all observers He took His place in the ranks. *Jesus wept.*

*Jesus wept* on this occasion, although it could have been misunderstood and misrepresented. Do you not think that the Jews who stood there would sneeringly say, "Look, He weeps! The miracle worker weeps! He calls Himself the Son of God, and yet He stands there weeping like any ordinary man!" This was opportunity for scorn at His apparent weakness, and even for blasphemy at the evident indication of it; but our Lord did not act upon policy. He allowed His true feeling to be seen. He did not act like the Stoic who would claim respect for his manhood by holding his emotions within himself and refusing to let people see that he was of similar feelings with them. No. *Jesus wept.*

Tears may not be thought manly, but they are natural to man, and Jesus would not be unnatural. His enemies can say what they please, and even blaspheme both Him and His God, but Jesus would not try to be anything other than He really was in the hope of silencing them. He acts the truth only, and weeps as His kind heart leads. He thinks more of Mary and Martha and the comfort His sympathy would bring them than of the coarse objections of unbelievers. The loving weakness of His humanity would forge an excuse for itself.

*Jesus wept*, and this reveals His love for Lazarus so much so that others saw it and cried, *See how He loved him!* (John 11:36). This is one proof that our Lord does not hesitate to declare His love to His people. When He sojourned upon earth, He was not ashamed to find friends among ordinary humans. Now that He is enthroned, our glorious Lord is not ashamed to call us brethren (Hebrews 2:11). He is not ashamed to be written down in the same heavenly record as His poor people. His cheeks were wet with tears, such as those that fall from our eyes, and by those tears everyone knew what manner of love He had toward His chosen. Blessed be His name! Many great men might be willing to be a friend to a poor man by giving a little money, but not by showing true tearful love; yet here the blessed Master, in the midst of the assembled multitude, acknowledges dead and rotting Lazarus as His friend, and He seals the covenant of His love with tears.

*Jesus wept.* He was not ashamed to acknowledge the distress that sin caused to His holy soul, nor the gash that the sight of death made in His heart. He could not bear to see the grave and its corruption. May we never think of the sin and misery of the human race without sorrow! I confess that I can never go through this huge city without feeling unhappy. I never pass from end to end of London without feeling a black and dark cloud hanging over my spirit like a cloth over a coffin.

How my heart breaks for you, O sinful city of London! Is it not so with you, my brethren? Think of your own city and its slums, its sins, its poverty, its ungodliness, its drunkenness, its corruption, its wickedness! These may well go through a person's heart like sharp swords. How Jesus would have wept in London! He could not stand in front of a lone grave, about to look upon a single corpse, without weeping. He saw in that one death the representation of what sin had done on so enormous a scale that it was impossible to compute the devastation; and therefore He wept.

What have you not done, O Sin! You have slain all these, O Death! What a field of blood has Satan made this earth! The Savior could not stand unmoved in the presence of the Destroyer, nor approach the gate of death's palace without deep emotion. He was by no means ashamed of this, and therefore He did not hold back His tears. *Jesus wept.* Brethren, holy emotion is not a weakness to be ashamed of. If at any time, in the midst of the world's wickedness and amusement, you weep, do not hide those tears! Let those who are thoughtless see that there is at least one person who fears God and trembles when the Holy One is provoked.

*Jesus wept*, even though He was about to work a wonderful miracle. The glory of His Godhead did not make Him ashamed of His manhood. It is a strange thing, too, that He would weep just before the joy of raising the dead to life. He is God, for He is about to call Lazarus out of the grave; but He is man just as much as ever, and therefore He weeps. Our Lord was as much man when He raised the dead as when He worked in the carpenter's shop at Nazareth. He was not ashamed to acknowledge His real manhood while He proved Himself to be the resurrection and the life.

This day in the glory of heaven He wears His scars to show that although He is God, He is not ashamed to be recognized as man. He makes this one of His glorious names: *I am . . . the living One; and I was dead, and behold, I am alive forevermore* (Revelation 1:17-18), thereby describing His connection with our manhood in life and in death. Beloved, *Jesus wept* to show that He did not scorn the feebleness of that nature that He had taken up so that He could redeem it unto God.

Remember that our Lord Jesus exercised three years of ministry, and each year was marked by a resurrection. He began by raising the little daughter of Jairus, upon whose unmarred countenance death had scarcely set its seal. Then He went on to raise the young man at the gates of Nain who was being carried out to his burial, dead but not yet corrupt. Now He makes His glory complete by raising Lazarus, who had already been dead four days. Yet when He came to this crowning marvel and thus displayed the perfection of His Godhead, He did not refuse to stand before all people and weep. Jesus is the Resurrection and the Life, yet *Jesus wept*.

### Thirdly, our Lord Jesus is our instructor in weeping.
This is the most practical part of our discourse. Be sure that you receive it by the teaching of the Holy Spirit.

Observe why Jesus wept, and learn a lesson from it. He wept because this was His method of prayer on this occasion. A great miracle was to be worked, and great power was needed from on high. As man, the Lord Jesus cried to God with intense earnestness and found the most proper expression for His prayer in this case in weeping. No prayer will ever prevail with God more certainly than a liquid petition that, being distilled from the heart, falls from the eye and waters the cheek. God is moved when He hears the voice of your weeping. The angel at Peniel will slip from your dry hands, but moisten them with tears, and you will hold him tight.

Before the Lord Jesus put forth the power that raised Lazarus from the grave, He appealed to God with strong crying and tears. The Father appeared for His weeping Son, and you, dear friends, if you want to win in prayer, must weep in prayer. Let your soul stir itself up to eager desire and trouble itself to anguish, and then you will prevail. *Jesus wept* to teach us how to baptize our prayers unto God in a wave of heart grief.

*Jesus wept* before He would awaken the dead because He would be stirred up Himself. A word of His could have worked the miracle; yes, His mere will would have been enough. But in order to instruct us, He did not make it so. There was a kind of evil that would not go out except by prayer and fasting (Matthew 17:21), and here was a kind of death that would not give up the dead unless the Savior groaned and wept. Without great exertion of the life of Jesus, the death in Lazarus could not be overcome. Therefore, the Lord stirred up all His strength, gathering all His energy for the struggle on which He entered.

Learn from this, my brother, that if you think to do any great good in saving sinners, you must not be half asleep yourself. You must be troubled even to tears. Perhaps the most difficult thing in winning souls is to get ourselves into a proper condition. The dead may bury the dead (Luke 9:60), but they cannot raise the dead. Until a person's entire soul is moved, he will not move his fellow man. He might possibly succeed with those who are willing to be influenced, but the careless will be unmoved by anyone who is unmoved himself. Tears storm a passage for warnings. If Christ's whole self must be stirred before Lazarus is raised, we must be awakened before we can win a soul.

The fingers of decay are unwinding the pleasant fabric that was once worn by the soul of Lazarus, and no voice can effectively command them to stop except one – that which sounds forth from a bursting heart. That stench of which Martha spoke can only be turned into the sweet odor of a grateful life by the salt tears of infinite love. It is even more so in our case. We must feel if others are to feel.

Come, my dear sister, you who are going to the Sunday school class this week because you must go. You must not go in that spirit. You, my brothers, who are going to preach or talk to your classes and have as yet only one eye open; this will never do. Your Lord was all alive and all sensitive, and you must be the same. How can you expect to see His power exercised on others if you do not feel His emotion in yourselves? You must be awakened into tenderness as He was, or you will not receive His life-giving power. *When I am weak, then I am strong* (2 Corinthians 12:10). *Jesus wept* when He raised dead Lazarus.

*Jesus wept* in full knowledge of several things that might have prevented His weeping. You have sometimes thought to yourself when weeping at the grave of a dear child, or wife, or husband, that you have been wrong in so doing; but this might not be the case. Our Savior wept, even though He knew that Lazarus was safe enough. I do not know what happened to the soul of Lazarus. It is not for me to speak where Scripture is silent. However, wherever he was, he was perfectly safe – and yet *Jesus wept*. Moreover, Jesus knew that He was going to raise Lazarus to life. His resurrection was close at hand – and yet *Jesus wept*. Sometimes we are told that if we really believed that our friends would rise again, and that they are safe and happy now, we should not weep. Why not? Jesus did. There cannot be any mistake by following where Jesus leads the way.

Jesus knew that the death of Lazarus was for the glory of God. He had said, *This sickness is not to end in death, but for the glory of God* (John 11:4), and yet He wept! Have we not thought that it must be wrong to weep when you know that the bereavement will glorify God? This is not true, or else Jesus would not have wept under similar circumstances. Learn instruction: tears that we might otherwise have considered to be prohibited now have free admission into the realm of holiness, since *Jesus wept*. Sister, you may weep, for *Jesus wept*. He wept with full knowledge of the happiness of Lazarus, with full expectation of his resurrection, and with the firm assurance that God was glorified even by his death. Let us not, therefore, condemn what Christ allows.

*Jesus wept*, but He did not sin. There was not even a particle of evil in any of the Redeemer's tears. There may have been salt, but there was no fault. Beloved, we can weep without sin. I do not suppose we have ever done so, but it is possible. It is not a sin to weep for those whom God has taken away from us, nor for those who are suffering. I will tell you why there was no sin in Christ's weeping: it was because He wept in His Father's presence. When He spoke in His sorrow, the first word was *Father.* He said, *Father, I thank You* (John 11:41). If you can weep in such a way that the entire time you feel God to be your Father, you can thank Him, and you know that you are in His presence, then your weeping is not blameworthy, but healthy. Let such floods flow on, for *Jesus wept,* and He said, *Father, I thank You.*

Brethren, we sin when we either laugh or weep behind God's back. Absence from God is the element of sin. When you cannot smile or weep except by forgetting God and His law, then you are offending; but if you can get up to your great Father's arms and bury your head in His chest, then you may sob away without restraint, for that which He allows is evidently no offense. *Jesus wept,* but He never complained. *Jesus wept,* but He never found fault with God's providence. *Jesus wept* sweetly in submission, not bitterly in rebellion.

I think there is good instruction in this. May the Holy Spirit teach it to us! May the Lord write it on every weeper's heart. You, Hannah, a woman of a sorrowful spirit, did Eli accuse you (1 Samuel 1:14)? Come to Eli's Master, the great High Priest, for He will not blame You. He will tell you that you may weep, for He also wept.

**I must be brief with my fourth point.** *Jesus wept.* **In this He is our comforter.**

Let me speak to those who are of heavy heart. *Jesus wept*; in this is our honor. You weep, my friend, in good company, for *Jesus wept.* Let no one condemn you in this, for they will not only be blaming you, but they will be blaming Jesus also.

*Jesus wept*; in this our sonship is vindicated. You ask, "Can I be a child of God and yet go on weeping?" Jesus was the wellbeloved Son, and yet He wept. We could ask the question another way: *What son is there whom his father does not discipline?* (Hebrews 12:7). What child did God ever have who did not weep? He had one Son without sin, but He never had a son without sorrow. He had a Son who never deserved a stroke of the rod, and yet against that Son the sword was awakened.

Mourner, you are one of the worshipful company of weepers of whom Jesus is the worthy Master. He is at the head of the clan of mourners.

You can well wear the plaid with the black and red crosses upon it, for your Leader wore the same.

See now the real sympathy of Christ with His people, for there is comfort in this. His sympathy lies not only in words, or even wholly in deeds; it is more tender than these can be. Only His heart could express His tender sympathy, and then it was by tears – tears that were brought up like gold from the ore bed of the heart, minted in the eyes, and then put in circulation as current coin of the merchant, each one bearing the King's image and superscription.

Jesus is our fellow sufferer, and this should be our greatest comfort. If we had a high priest who did not know what it was to suffer as we do, it would be a most unhappy thing for us! If we fled to him for refuge and learned that he never known any grief and sorrow, and so could not relate to us, it would be death to our broken hearts. I saw a young bird flying yesterday who thought he had a clear path, but sadly for him, there was an invisible barrier. He flew into the glass and stunned himself, and I was sad when I saw him lying dead outside my window.

If in my grief I fled to Jesus, and there was about Him a secret inability to sympathize and an incapacity to admit me to His heart, then even though that barrier might be as pure as crystal, I would dash myself against it and die in despair. A Jesus who never wept could never wipe away my tears. That would be a grief I could not bear – if He could not have fellowship with me and could not understand my suffering and sorrow!

Beloved, think how bravely our Lord endured, for in this there is confidence. Tears did not drown the Savior's hope in God. He lived. He triumphed, notwithstanding all His sorrow. Because He lives, we will live also (John 14:19). He says, *Take courage; I have overcome the world* (John 16:33). Though our hero had to weep in the fight, He was not defeated. He came, He wept, and He conquered. You and I share much in common with Jesus. We share the tears of His eyes, and we will share the diamonds of His crown. We wear the crown of thorns here, and we will wear the crown of glory hereafter.

Let this comfort you, too, that even though He wept, He weeps no more; in this, heaven is begun here below. *Death no longer is master over Him* in any sense or degree (Romans 6:9). He is done weeping. It will be that way with us before long. How I love that promise: *There will no longer be any mourning, or crying, or pain* (Revelation 21:4). Heaven is without a temple, for it is all devotion. It is without a hospital, for it is all health and love. *No resident will say, "I am sick"* (Isaiah 33:24).

I look greatly forward to the no more weeping! It will come to us before long, for it has come to Jesus. The Lord God *will wipe away every tear from their eyes* (Revelation 21:4). We will soon have no cause for sorrow and no possibility of grief, for as He is, so we will be. Just as He is perfectly blessed, so we will be blessed in Him. *Jesus wept*, but His weeping is all over. *Jesus wept*, but His sorrow is now a thing of the past, and so will ours be before long.

**Fifthly and lastly, *Jesus wept*, and in this He is our example.**
We should weep, for *Jesus wept*. *Jesus wept* for others. I do not know that He ever wept for Himself. His tears were sympathetic tears. He embodied that command, *Weep with those who weep* (Romans 12:15). He who can hold it all within the compass of his ribs has a narrow soul. A true soul, a Christly soul, lives in other men's souls and bodies as well as in its own. A perfectly Christly soul finds all the world too narrow for its abode, for it lives and loves. It lives by loving, and it loves because it lives.

Think of other weepers, and have pity upon those who are grieving. Today I want to touch your heartstrings and move you to pity the pains and agonies of the many who are now lying in our hospitals, and the even greater miseries of those who languish for lack of medicine and care because they cannot get into the hospitals, but have to wear themselves out in hopeless disease. How they must suffer who have bad nursing and little food, and in the winter are afflicted with cold! You and I may never suffer as they do, but at least let us grieve on their behalf and stand ready to help them to the best of our ability.

Our Lord is our example in another way, too. Let us learn from Him that our indignation against evil will best show itself in compassion for sinners. Ah, my dear friend! I heard you lecturing tremendously against drunkenness. I am glad to hear you do so. You cannot say anything too hard or too heavy about that degrading vice, but I ask you to end your denunciation by weeping over the poor drunkard.

I heard you speak, my other friend, on behalf of the League of Purity, and you smote the monsters of lust and immorality with all your force. I wish more strength to your arm! But when you have finished, sit down and weep over such filthiness that should defile men and women who are your fellow creatures.

Appeal to Congress, if you want, to make laws to stop sin, but Congress itself first needs correcting and purifying. A flood of tears before the thrice Holy God will do far more than the greatest number of petitions to our politicians. *Jesus wept*, and His tears were mighty weapons against sin and death. You feel angry at the lazy, idle, loafing vagabonds whose very difficulties are produced by their own iniquity. I cannot condemn your virtuous wrath, but if you want to imitate Jesus in all things, please note that it is not written that Jesus thundered, but that *Jesus wept*.

Let indignation have sympathy mixed with it. I do not like lightning without rain, nor indignation without tears. I know what you will say about the lack of frugality among the poor, about the absence of sobriety, the lack of hard work, and so forth. Admit all this sorrowfully, rebuke it tenderly, and then weep. You will do more good to the offenders, more good to yourself, and more good to the best of causes if tears of compassion and sympathy moisten it all. You can, if you want, beat the dreadful drum and sound the trumpet of war, but the noise will deafen rather than soften. The voice of your weeping will be heard deep down in the soul, and it will work more wonders than thunders of denunciation.

Lastly, when you have wept, imitate your Savior and do something! If the eleventh chapter of John had finished with *Jesus wept*, it would have been a poor ending. If, after they had come to the grave, we had read "Jesus wept, and then went about His daily business," I would not have much comfort in the passage. If nothing had come of it except tears, it would have been a great decline from the usual ways of our blessed Lord.

Tears! By themselves, they are only salt water. A cup of them would not be worth much to anyone. But, beloved, *Jesus wept*, and then He commanded, *Remove the stone* (John 11:39). He cried, *Lazarus, come forth* (John 11:43). When Lazarus struggled out of the tomb, Jesus said, *Unbind him, and let him go* (John 11:44). Some of you are full of sympathy for the sick, but I hope that not does end in mere emotion. Do not let us say, "We were moved to sympathize with the sick, but we did not do much to help them." I would be ashamed to think that this would be so.

If you cannot raise the dead, give something toward rolling away the stone that prevents the poor from getting medical help. If you cannot restore them to health, at least do something toward removing their sickness and trouble. Comfort them. Help them. Feed them. Clothe them. Pay their bills. Find something to do. Brethren, in this way we can practically prove the truth of our sympathy. Give generously!

## Chapter 8

# Might Have Been, or May Be

> *Some of them said, "Could not this man, who opened the eyes of the blind man, have kept this man also from dying?"* (John 11:37)

*J*esus wept. That does not mean that He shed a tear or two, but that His tears flowed freely. That is the meaning gained from the original word. Jesus wept profusely and continuously until all who observed Him knew that He was deeply affected. His tears were the suitable expression of His intense emotion.

Love made Him weep. Nothing else ever compelled Him to tears. I do not find that all the pains He endured, even when scourged or when fastened to the cruel tree, produced a single tear from Him; but for love's sake *Jesus wept*. At first I feel inclined to say, "See how He wept!" Then I stop myself, borrow my language from the bystanders, and I say, *See how He loved him!* (John 11:36). Even with their unfriendly eyes, the Jews recognized that His tears were drawn from Him by love alone. From this Rock of our salvation, no rod except that of love could bring forth floods of water.

So when we have noticed the tears and the power of love that brought forth the tears, let us observe that tears are an expression of His love toward us. When you look upon your children with love, your eyes flash with joy. When they are in health and strength, your love expresses itself properly in delight in them. But with Christ, love toward us most properly shows itself in tears. When He thinks of what we are, how we have become subject to death, and how sin has brought us under this bondage, He must weep because He loves us. Even more, He must die, for even His tears cannot suffice to demonstrate His love. Jesus must pour out His soul, not only unto tears, but unto death, so that all may see how deeply He loves us.

I want to begin this section with that thought deeply fixed upon our spirits: if we are indeed the people of God, then Jesus loves us, and He loves us unto tears. Since we see how He loved Lazarus when Lazarus was dead and in the tomb, let us now see how He loved us when we were dead in trespasses and sins (Ephesians 2:1). See how He loves us even though our spirits might be dull and dead, and how He will love us even when we come to die. *Precious in the sight of the LORD is the death of His godly ones* (Psalm 116:15). He loves us in such a way that He will love us when we die, even as He loved Lazarus at the grave's mouth.

Let us turn away from our preface, which we have found in the context, and look at the text itself. While there were some who thought only of the love of Christ when they saw His tears, there were others standing by who were more full of reasoning and who wondered, *Could not this man, who opened the eyes of the blind man, have kept this man also from dying?* (John 11:37).

Looking at the text from different perspectives, I see a vain argument, a vile argument, a fair argument, and, if read in connection with the verses that follow it, a full and faithful argument.

**First, I see in the text a vain argument.**
It is an argument about what might have been if such-and-such a thing had been. It is a very common thing to hear people talk this way: "If this would have happened, then that might have occurred." Such talk is always vain and foolish because it does not lead to any practical result. What was the use of saying, "If Jesus had been here, then Lazarus would not have died," when Lazarus was already dead? The thing is done, and it cannot be undone. What is the use of asking about what once might have been but now cannot be?

Yet I have seen strange sorrows twisted out of these suppositions.

Sometimes the bitterest griefs that people know do not come from facts, but from things they imagine might have been. That is to say, they dig wells of supposition and drink the bitter waters of regret. The sisters of Lazarus did this. Each one said, *Lord, if You had been here, my brother would not have died* (John 11:21, 32). In a more unbelieving way, the Jews asked, *Could not this man, who opened the eyes of the blind man, have kept this man also from dying?* Yes, and so you say, "If I had gone to so-and-so, this would not have happened; and then the other might have happened; and a third thing probably would have occurred; and then how different it would have been from what it is now!" You blame yourself for steps that were not only innocent, but were wise and right; but now that you see the consequences of them, you begin to imagine that they were not innocent, not wise, and not right, and you regret that you took such steps.

I have known some go a great deal further than vainly accusing themselves; they have even accused God. They say, "Why was moral evil allowed into the world? Why were men and women made as they are? Could not God, who is omnipotent, have arranged things so that there would have been no sin and no sorrow?"

What a big mess we get into once we begin arguing over those points and supposing what might have been under other circumstances! You see, dear friends, these things will not be, and they cannot be; therefore, what good does it do to worry over what is not and what cannot be? I will plow, but if there is not a field, I hope you will excuse me. I will not plow the sea or the mist. I will get to work on anything that is practical, but I will not break my heart over daydreams.

If it is to be done and if it is right to do, then let's get to it at once; but if it cannot be done now but is only something that might have been, then let us leave it alone. You can go to the "might have beens," but I have better work to do. This was David's method regarding his child, and it should be yours regarding all your sick ones, as well as those who have already departed. David fasted, prayed, and cried to God as long as his child was alive, but when his child was dead, he washed his face and ate bread, saying, *Can I bring him back again? I will go to him, but he will not return to me* (2 Samuel 12:23). It is done and cannot be undone. What is the use of worrying about it now?

Oh, that you would have grace to leave this foolish chopping of logic with yourself and providence, using your reason for something better! Lazarus is dead; what is the use of saying that he might not have died if Jesus had been there?

Another reason that this is a vain argument is because even though we ask about what might have been, and we consider it until we begin to think that it should have been, unbelief will still never get an explanation about it from the Lord. In this chapter of the Bible, there is no explanation given to the Jews of why Jesus, who was able to open the eyes of the blind man and was able to prevent Lazarus from dying, did not keep him from dying. An explanation was given by the Lord to His disciples by His assurance that it was for the glory of God. That explanation you will get. You have received it already. If you are God's child, and He has denied to you what you think He could have given you, or if He has permitted you to suffer under a calamity that you think He could have averted, He will give you no other explanation than the one He gives you now without any pressure at all – that it is for His glory. If it is for His glory, is it not for your advantage? What can more profit a servant than the glory of his master? What can more profit our loving hearts than to see God glorified? If you are not satisfied with that answer, do not expect any other.

"Why have I been bereaved of my children?" "Why have I been sick for so many years?" "Why did I fail when I hoped to be successful?" "Why did I not do well in pursuing a college education?" It is a useless piece of business to demand the reasons for unavoidable trials. It is mere dreaming to guess what would have been if something else had happened. *What I do you do not realize now, but you will understand hereafter* (John 13:7). Be content with that.

This is also a vain argument because it cannot benefit you to try to look into that which the Lord has hidden from you. You are promoting self-conceit in judging God's providence. You are practically sitting upon a throne and making God the prisoner at your judgment seat. You are considering again what He has already determined in the scale of His wisdom. This will never do.

A childlike spirit is infinitely healthier and infinitely holier than the spirit of questioning. Brothers, we should not even desire to know all the things that are, for if it is the glory of God to conceal something, let it be concealed. As for the things that might have been, what have we to do with them? If we begin lifting up these curtains, we cannot tell what we may one day see. I have known people intrude into this sphere until at last they have stumbled on a horror that they were never intended to see, and which indeed they never would have seen if their own unholy imaginations had not created it for themselves. They were ambitious to change the ways of God and to change the times and seasons that God had ordained, and at last they fell into such a dismal condition that, if they were not completely insane, they would have been happier if they had been, for there is a state of mind bordering on insanity that still has a guilt about it, and is therefore worse than if responsibility had been destroyed.

I will beg you, therefore, brethren, to abstain from trying to look into those secret things that belong to God only (Deuteronomy 29:29). It is beneficial for you to abstain from such speculations. Do not talk about what might have been or should have been, interfering with the good that God has given you by yearning after what He has denied. Oh, if you could know as He knows, and then love as He loves, you would act as He acts! Believe in Him, sit still at His feet, and do not talk anymore about what He could have done or might have done or what you think He should have done, lest evil come of it.

**Second, I see in the text a vile argument.**
I believe these Jews intended a kind of evil argument against the Christ of God. They put it this way: this Man says that He opened the eyes of the blind, and all the people think that He did; but if He did so, why would He not keep His friend, whom He evidently loved, from dying? Either He lacks power, which will prove that He did not open the eyes of the blind after all, but that it was a hoax, or else if He has such power and does not use it for His friend, He does not love him, and these tears are a mere show. He could have saved this man's life, and now He stands here and weeps because he is dead.

Thus, the adversary desired to put those who believe in our Lord upon the horns of a dilemma. We are not gored by either horn, for we know a way of escape. Still you see the intent, and this is often the pattern of Satan's arguments. Your brother, your mother, your child, your friend – they are dead. You called to Jesus, you cried to God, you begged for the precious life – yet they are dead. Well, then, there must have been a lack of power on the part of God to save life. Maybe your conversion, in which you have rejoiced and of which you have said, *One thing I do know, that though I was blind, now I see* (John 9:25) – maybe that was not a work of divine power after all, but was only a delusion. He who saved your soul could have saved the life of your beloved, and as He did not do so, does He have any power at all, and have you ever seen His power in your own life?

You see the pattern of the misleading reasoning; is it not a vile argument? Let us unveil the falsehood of it. Suppose that Jesus is willing to open the eyes of the blind, and that He does open them. Is He therefore obligated to raise this particular dead man? If He does not see fit to do so, does that prove that He does not have the power to do so? If He lets Lazarus die, is that proof that He could not have saved his life? Could there not be some other reason? Does the omnipotent God always exert His power? Does He ever exert all His power? Could there not be some great reason why Christ would open the eyes of the blind, and yet not step in to prevent the death of Lazarus? We can see that there could be many such reasons, but it is easy, when you want to argue against Christ and the gospel, to forget much. You can shut your eyes where it is inconvenient to see, and then you can rush on blindly like a mad bull.

On the other hand, they might say, "If Christ can prevent Lazarus from dying, and He does not do so, there is a lack of love in Him." Is that true? Is that a fair argument? It is not true as a matter of fact, nor will it be thought to be true by our faith. It might be infinite love that wounds, chastens, and afflicts. There is as much love in the Father when He uses the rod of correction as when He gives the kiss of affection. There is as much love in the Savior when He allows Lazarus to die as when He raises Lazarus from the grave. Yes, and it is possible that the less-pleasing deed can be the one more greatly filled with love!

The greatest blessings come to us in the form of sorrows. I would not wonder if the death of Lazarus resulted in the passing of Lazarus into a higher state of spiritual life than he had ever known before. I do not doubt that he was a converted man before his death, but certainly that wonderful passing into the region of death and coming back again must have given him such a vivid consciousness of the power of Christ that the spiritual life within him must have become more strong, more clear, and more supreme than it had ever been before.

I would have liked to have met that man after he had been raised from the dead by Him who said, *I am the resurrection and the life.* I think he could have preached from that text very wonderfully. He would have understood it by an experience unknown to us. I would think that Lazarus rose into the higher life in the very highest degree, and so it was Christ's love to Lazarus that let Lazarus die, and it was a completely wicked misrepresentation to say that Lazarus died because Jesus had a lack of love toward him. It is Christ's love that has let some of you be sick and poor. It is Christ's love that has allowed you to be despised and downtrodden. It is Christ's love that has let you remain in affliction, because the divine benefit that has come from it is more to your profit than the affliction itself could ever be to your loss. So the vile argument may well be driven away, whatever shape it takes in our minds.

There is no justification for us not to trust what God has done for us in the way of grace. It has been real, and was no dream. There is no justification for any doubt as to what God can do for us and will do for us in the future. He who has helped us so far will help us to the end. He who has done so much for us will withhold no good thing from us (Psalm 84:11), but will give to us all that is needful for this life and godliness (2 Peter 1:3), and for the life to come and glory (Romans 8:18; 1 Timothy 4:8).

**Third, I see in the text a very fair argument.**
If you take the text and press the animosity out of it, it is true: *Could not this man, who opened the eyes of the blind man, have kept this man also from dying?* Yes, it is true. Jesus Christ, by what He has done, has proved His power to do anything. I do not need to expand upon the point, but I will briefly mention it. There is not a life that He cannot preserve. You may cry to Him about your sick ones. You are permitted to do so. Even if the physician has given up hope, I counsel you to go to Jesus about them, even though it is far better to go to Jesus before you consult the physician. We often make a mistake about the use of

medicines by using medicine first. We should go to the Lord first so that we can be guided as to what medicine and method should be used, and we should trust in God to bless the means made use of for healing and restoration.

We can make idols out of physicians as much as the heathen make idols out of blocks of wood. Medicines are proper enough in their place for healing, just as bread is good for nourishment; but just as people cannot live by bread alone (Matthew 4:4), so they are not healed by medicine alone. Before we eat bread, we should ask God's blessing on that bread; let us also seek a blessing on medicines whenever we use them. We are not healed by the physician, but by that God who works according to His own will and pleasure (Philippians 2:13). Let us then believe that the Christ, who has done this and that for other sick people, can do the same for those whom we bring to Him, and let us leave their cases in His hands.

Now look at the text spiritually. I want you to believe that Christ can preserve us spiritually from death. Are we forced by our employment into the society of the ungodly? Does providence call some of you working people to labor side by side, or even at the same bench, with wicked unbelievers? The Lord Jesus can keep you from being harmed by them. He can give you spiritual health and strength, even when you seem to be under the most deadly influences. He who opened your eyes when you were blind can keep you alive now that you can see. Trust in Him for your final perseverance with the same unquestioning faith with which you trusted in Him for the forgiveness of your sin.

I say again that He who opened your eyes when you were in darkness can keep you from death even if the deadliest influences from the world, the flesh, and the devil would be set in operation against you. Because He lives, you will live also (John 14:19). Run to Him in the time of your temptation. Cry to Him in the hour of your need. He will help you and deliver you. You will not die, but will live and declare the works of the Lord (Psalm 118:17).

Beloved, what mercy it is that we can look back upon Christ's having opened the blind man's eyes and see the same thing in ourselves! Here is a blind man whose eyes Christ opened. It is you. He was able to give you sight, and can you not make the same claim to others? If the Lord Jesus Christ could give you sight, He can give sight to others. If He opened your blind eyes, He can open the blind eyes of your children, your unconverted father, your unsaved brothers, and your unsaved sisters.

Believe that God can open the eyes of your friends, and cry to God about them. Take the text at once, and read it like this: "Could not this Man, who opened my blind eyes, open the blind eyes of those about whom my heart is heavy?" Remember that the man who was blind, whose eyes Christ opened, was born blind. Christ can deal with original sin and natural sin. Some seem to have inherited a nature that is more wild than common. Their heart does not appear to be a heart of flesh, but a heart of stone; yet Jesus, who dealt with this man who was blind from his birth, can deal with those strange sinners, those sinners of a scarlet color, who develop a more desperate viciousness in their lives than you see in others. Christ can deal with the most wicked sinners. Take them to Him, believe on account of them, and be fully convinced that no case is beyond the power of the living Savior.

As for me, I never can or will despair of the salvation of one of my fellow creatures now that I am myself saved. I know that there were certain traits in my character and certain elements in my temperament that make my conversion to Christ more remarkable than that of the conversion of many others, and so I will have hope concerning the most blasphemous, the most obstinate, and the most unbelieving people. This glorious Man who, in the days of His flesh, opened the eyes of one born blind, a thing that had never been known before (Mark 2:12), can come and deal with the very chief of sinners! He can deal with sinners who are dead in sin and who lie rotting in their sinful pleasures – and He can make them to be saints! This is a fair argument; I am sure it is.

**Lastly, there is a full and faithful argument from the text.**
All they said was that this Man, who has opened the eyes of one born blind, could have prevented Lazarus from dying. That was a fair argument, but it was not a full argument. It never occurred to them to go further and ask, "Now that Lazarus is dead, cannot this Man raise him from the dead?" The first piece of argument did not go far enough to provide any comfort, because it only dealt with what might have been

and what could not be. I am afraid that a great deal of our religion is of that kind. What mercy it would be if God would give some Christians two cents' worth of common sense!

Oh, if some people could only believe what I am sure is true – that the true Christian religion is sanctified common sense, that the religion of Jesus Christ is just as practical as if our life were to be spent in running a business! True, it is spiritual and divine, heavenly and sublime, but it is as accurate as if we were to be nothing but mathematicians, calculating and estimating all our days. There is a mathematical truthfulness about our holy faith, as well as a lofty, eagle-winged ambition.

Therefore, they should have argued like this: "Jesus Christ, who opened this blind man's eyes, has come to a corpse in its grave, and He is able to make it live." Friend, is there laid upon your mind at this time some poor sinner who is dead in trespasses and sins? You cannot get at him. You don't know how to make him feel or think. There does not seem to be a vital spark anywhere about him, and you don't know how to deal with him. Believe that the gospel is meant for such a case as this, and that the living God, in Jesus Christ, by the Holy Spirit, can meet with this stone-cold dead heart.

"Oh, it is worse than that," you say. "It is worse than that. The person I am thinking of is put out of society and is too corrupt to be spoken with." Yes, I know what you mean. Maybe you are speaking of a fallen woman. We are always more eager to bury the fallen women than the fallen men. A man, of whom we must say with Martha, *By this time there will be a stench* (John 11:39), may still be tolerated in society; but if it happens to be a woman who sins, they cry, "Bury her out of sight. Roll the stone to the mouth of the tomb. We will never speak to her or mention her." If you have concern in your soul about a person who is shut out from society in this way, I want you to believe that Jesus can bring out the buried and corrupt.

"Oh!" you say, "but it is not just that the person I am thinking of is buried away, but the situation is really one that cannot be described. He has been dead four days. He has gone so far that his crime cannot even be mentioned." I know the case. Yet you can still mention it before the Lord. No harm will come of it in His presence. I do not read in the gospel narrative of anybody being bothered by the odor when the sepulcher of Lazarus was opened. When Jesus said, *Remove the stone,* He knew that He had divine disinfectants ready at hand.

He knew what He did. When you seek after flagrant sinners, prudent people say, "Well, if you go after such people as that, your own character will be tarnished before long." The Lord will prevent any harm coming from it, for He can speak to the most corrupt sinner, and say, "Live," and he will live; then the corruption is no more. Therefore, let us drive out of our minds the idea that any sinner is too far gone for Christ to save him. I used to hear in my youth about a "day of grace," and about people having passed that day of grace, but I do not believe it. As long as you are in this world, I am told to preach to you, for the gospel message is to be proclaimed to every creature, and I dare not draw empty distinctions about a day of grace.

If you have a disease that will carry you off before midnight tonight, I still urge you to believe in Christ and live. If you are so bad in your own opinion that there never lived a worse man or a worse woman outside of hell, I still plead with you to believe in Jesus Christ. My Lord loves to save great sinners, just as He delighted to bring from the grave the long-dead Lazarus so that he could be received into the arms of his family, to be the joy of the house and the glory of Christ.

I have not gone too far. I am sure that I have not. No, I could not go too far. The shoreless, bottomless love of my great Lord – I wish I had the tongues of men and angels to tell of it. You have not sinned beyond His power to save you. He is a great Savior and a mighty Savior, and His precious blood can remove all your death and corruption. When I think of those whom He has saved, I argue, "Could not my Lord Jesus, who opened the eyes of the blind, make these dead sinners live?"

I will tell you something else. If you are that dead sinner, I say to you, in the name of Jesus Christ of Nazareth, *Believe in the Lord Jesus, and you will be saved* (Acts 16:31).

"I cannot believe," someone says, "for I am dead." I know that you are, but if the Lord speaks to you, you will live; and He does speak to you through this voice of mine. I speak to you in His name. You careless sinner, in the name of Jesus Christ of Nazareth, consider your ways! You dead sinner, in the name of Jesus, live! His Spirit has gone forth with the word that I have spoken. The thing has already been done in some who have heard me – the spiritually dead have been brought to life – and it will be done in others who will read these words. Glory be to the Father, and to the Son, and to the Holy Spirit, forever and ever! Amen.

## Chapter 9

# The Sphere of Instrumentality

*Jesus said, "Remove the stone."* (John 11:39)

*Jesus said to them, "Unbind him, and let him go"* (John 11:44). There lay Lazarus in the grave – dead. His restoration to life was utterly hopeless by any ordinary principles. Certainly Lazarus could not raise himself. His loving sisters could not, with all their weeping, give him a resurrection, nor could the disciples call back the departed spirit and reanimate the decaying corpse. It was a hopeless case, for who could revive a dead man who had lain in the grave so long that he had begun to stink?

This is a similar case to that of every unconverted sinner in the world. He is dead in trespasses and sins (Ephesians 2:1). He is not just a little sick, lightly wounded, or has fainted, but spiritual death reigns over him. The sinner never gives life to himself. That is inconceivable. There are people who think that the natural will of man sometimes leans toward good, but, sadly, this pleasing thought is far from the truth. Jesus said, *You are unwilling to come to Me so that you may have life* (John 5:40). People are not any more desirous to come now than they did then.

Until we see dead people raising themselves, we do not expect to meet with sinners who have spontaneously and without divine assistance turned themselves toward righteousness. Nor can relatives or friends regenerate someone else's soul. Even the most earnest ministers cannot give out the spirit that makes the dead live. Those whom God has blessed in the past are still quite powerless in any new situation unless the same power works in and through them once again.

Death is a terrible picture of our natural state, but it is by no means an exaggerated one. The whole world lies before us as a valley of dry bones, according to Ezekiel's vision (Ezekiel 37), and if the dry bones are ever to live, it will not be through an energy that is naturally found within themselves. It will not be through a power residing in the most zealous people, or even through any power that a prophet has apart from God. Education cannot develop life out of death, persuasion cannot produce it there, and reasoning cannot bring it about. The divine arm must be revealed, or the case is without hope.

Jesus must come to the tomb of Lazarus, and His voice must cry out, *Lazarus, come forth* (John 11:43), or else the corpse will remain lifeless and will increase in decay. All that can be done by mortal man may be done, but nothing will be accomplished unless Jesus, who is the resurrection and the life, will speak the life-giving word. The power lies in His omnipotent voice, and only there. Let this be taken as a plain statement of our belief as to the Lord's work in salvation, and let it be taken without any softening or dilution: we believe that in every case, salvation is of the Lord alone and entirely. Regeneration is a supernatural work. We must be born again from above; any power less than power from heaven will be futile. The new creation is as much and entirely the work of God as the old creation.

> Can aught beneath a power divine
> The stubborn will subdue?
> 'Tis thine, Eternal Spirit, thine
> To form the heart anew.
>
> To chase the shades of death away,
> And bid the sinner live;
> A beam of heaven, a vital ray,
> 'Tis thine alone to give.[18]

---

18  This is from a hymn by Anne Steele that begins with "How helpless guilty nature lies."

Having said this, we proceed to bear witness that what can be done by us should be done, since what can be done by man will not be done by Christ. It is a rule with our Lord never to work needless miracles. Indeed, He only begins the miraculous when the ordinary means can go no further. He follows the ordinary up to its threshold, and then the extraordinary comes in.

If a multitude needs to be fed, as long as there are barley loaves and fish available, Jesus will use them. He will multiply them and make them go further than they naturally could, but He will use them as far as they will go. If there had not been any bread or fish, I do not doubt that He would have embarked upon an act of creation, but since there were a few loaves and some fish, He did not ignore them, but made them the basis of a work of multiplication (John 6:1-14).

What a person can do for himself, God will not do for him. What Christians can do for sinners, they must not expect the Lord to do. They must themselves do what can be done according to the ability God has given them up to the point of possibility, and then they can look for divine intervention.

Observe in this situation that there was a stone in front of the mouth of the cave in which Lazarus was buried. Could not our Lord have removed that stone with a word? Could He not have said, "Roll away, O stone," and it would have been done? Yes, He could have consumed the stone with a glance if He had wanted to, but He did not choose to do so, because the bystanders were quite able to move the stone. Therefore He said to them, *Remove the stone.*

When Lazarus was raised, when he had come forth from the hole in which his friends had laid him, he was clothed with the garments of the tomb; rolls of linen were around his body, and a cloth was around his head. Jesus did not remove the clothing of the grave by divine power. It would have been a smaller miracle, if miracles can be compared, to loose the living with a word than it was to awaken the dead, but since it could be done without a miracle, it was done without a miracle. Jesus said to those who stood by, *Unbind him, and let him go.*

The analogy teaches us that there are some things that we can do for the unconverted and that we are obligated to do for them. There are certain other ways in which we can aid those who are newly converted, and these we should be quick to do. While we look only to the life-giving Lord to give life to the soul, we do not fold our arms in indifference or excuse ourselves from all effort because we say we are unable to do anything, but we are to be watching to see where human means are applicable. We should be ready at all times to be made useful wherever and however we can. We cannot turn the dry bones into living people, but we can proclaim God's Word to them and, blessed be God, we can also preach to the four winds (Ezekiel 37:9), and so by these means the dead may live.

The subject now is the sphere of human action in connection with regeneration. *Help us, O Divine Spirit.* First, there are some things that we can do for the unconverted before they are given new life. Jesus said, *Remove the stone* (John 11:39). Second, there are some things that we can do for them after they have been made alive in Christ. Jesus said, *Unbind him, and let him go* (John 11:44).

**First, then, dear brethren, there are some things that we can do for the unconverted before they are given new life.**
I am sure, if our hearts are right, we are very anxious to do all that can be done. Jesus Christ is our example, and observe how He labored in the work of blessing the sons of men. In this case He took a long journey, He wept, He groaned, He was troubled in spirit, He prayed, and then He spoke loudly. This is a true picture of what every Christian should be, and especially every Christian minister. We should journey after souls. We should weep over their ruined condition. We should groan for them and be troubled in heart on their account. We should be incessant in our prayers, and when God speaks through us to the those who are dead in sins, it should not be with lighthearted tones, but with a voice tender of love and passionate with zeal. We are to be imitators of Christ in this. We should throw our whole heart into the blessed work that He honors us to do in His name.

Brethren, we can all do for the ungodly what the sisters did for their brother. Mary and Martha called in the Master to minister to their sorrow. Being well assured when their brother was ill that they had no more sympathizing or capable friend in all the world than the Master whom they loved, they sent a message to Jesus. Although they did not send a second message afterward, I do not doubt that they felt that the first message was enough. So you and I, in the case of all the unconverted over whom our spirit yearns, should call the Savior to the rescue.

Let us send a message to Him about them. You can word it in such a way as this: "O Lord, I grieve to tell You that my dear child is still unsaved," or "Lord, You know that my heart breaks because my wife (or husband) is still unconverted," or "O Savior, You know that there are children in my Sunday school class who have not yet been brought to You," or "My God, You know that I have preached to many of these people for many years, and yet they are still unmoved and remain strangers to their God." We must earnestly intercede with the Lord for souls. Jesus can work wonders. He is the resurrection and the life, and our wisdom is to lay hold upon His strength and to plead with Him to reveal His saving might.

In addition to this, we must then express our confident faith in Jesus – that even now God will give to Him whatsoever He will ask of God. We must believe that He is able to raise the spiritually dead. We must never allow ourselves to despair of anyone since the matter is in the hands of an Almighty Savior. Although by this time the sinner has a stench (John 11:39) and has become immoral, as well as unholy, it is not too late to ask the Lord Jesus to work. We should never say of anyone, "It would be vain for us to labor for his conversion, for he is so evil as to be incapable of grace." We are not merely to await man's condemnation, but rather we are to obey the Master's message and go into all the world with good news for every person (Matthew 28:19), for the gospel is without limitation when it declares that he who believes and is baptized will be saved (Mark 16:16).

Beloved, have faith in the Lord Jesus. Tell Him how desperate the situation is for you, but say to Him, "Lord, it is not impossible with You." Tell Him that while you feel that you have no power yourself, you are sure that one single word from Him will accomplish all that your soul desires.

Every believer can do this. With God's help, we can go by faith to the Lord Jesus. But our first text indicates even more clearly that we have a part to play. Jesus employed others to roll away the stone. You cannot make the dead live, but you can take the stone away from their sepulcher. Let us now look at certain stones that we should remove with all diligence.

The first is the stone of ignorance. This heavy weight lies at the mouth of many spiritual graves at this day. I think we take for granted too high an attainment of knowledge among the people at this present time. I am sure that many sermons are preached to people as though they perfectly understood the plan of salvation, but if the preacher knew his hearers better, he would learn that many of them are deplorably ignorant even about the basic elements of the gospel of Christ. In fact, I am afraid that the elementary truths of Christianity are not preached sufficiently often because too much is taken for granted.

It is to be feared that the basics of the gospel are unknown to thousands whose teachers are trying to instruct them in the classics of theology – a waste of effort and a dangerous experiment. Even in this city you will find people who frequently attend Protestant churches who still believe in salvation by their own works and are horrified at justification by faith. You will discover, if you go among the people, such a large indifference to salvation that it is appalling – and this originates largely in ignorance. Salvation! Thousands do not know what you mean by the term, and here, in this century of light and advancement as we boastfully call it, thick darkness covers the minds of a large proportion of our countrymen.

Brethren, the time has not come for you to stop distributing the very plainest gospel tracts. The time has not arrived for you to be silent at the street corners about the first principles of the faith. You must still proclaim atonement by the sacrifice of Christ and the simple doctrine of justification by faith. There might possibly come an age when it will be wise to talk mainly upon the deep things of God, but for this present distress, we can wisely give our whole strength to telling out the foundational fact – that *Christ Jesus came into the world to save sinners* (1 Timothy 1:15).

Our sermons should often tell the story of the cross. The hymns most commonly sung should be those such as "Rock of ages, cleft for me," "Jesus, lover of my soul," "Come, ye sinners, poor and wretched," and "Just as I am, without one plea." We even have need of such simple songs as "I do believe, I will believe, that Jesus died for me." Upon that basic point, ignorance and unbelief still cloud the majority of the people among whom we dwell.

Let not the people be *destroyed for lack of knowledge* (Hosea 4:6). Let none go down to hell because they do not know of the Savior. Let me say here that even with those who have heard the gospel preached often, this ignorance may still remain, as it did in my own case. I believe that if I had known that all I had to do was to look to Christ and I would live, if I had really understood that there was nothing for me to be, feel, or do, but that I only had to rest in a finished work and take from God's mercy that which Christ had completed, I think I would have found peace with God sooner. However, I did not understand the gospel, and therefore remained in distress of mind. Do, then, tell everybody about Jesus. Tell them about the Son of God made flesh. Tell them about Christ dying in our place. Speak this word plainly. Tell them:

> He bore that we might never bear
>  His Father's righteous ire.[19]

Assure them that whosoever believes in Jesus is not condemned, and that to believe is to trust. Then explain it further, for even plain and simple words can get to be technical, and people imagine that there is some other meaning in them than that which they usually have. You cannot put the gospel too plainly, but in any case, do put it before them, and in this way roll away this stone from the mouth of the sepulcher.

A second stone is the stone of absolute error. It is not good for the mind to be without knowledge, for if we do not sow wheat, weeds will certainly spring up. People ignorant of God's righteousness always go about to establish their own righteousness in some way or other (Romans 10:3). Thousands think that if they are sincere, honest, upright, and so on, they have done all that is required of them. They think that a little church attendance and some religious ceremonies can squeeze any deficiencies of their lives. Certainly to call in a pastor or minister when they are dying, and to have prayers said or read to them, will complete the process that they have themselves begun, they think.

---

19  This is from a hymn by Augustus Toplady that begins with "O Thou who didst Thy glory leave."

Brethren, this great stone covers many graves; seek to roll it away. Bear your own personal protest against the idea that the law of God will ever be satisfied by an imperfect obedience. Teach people that God's commandment is exceedingly broad and that it deals with the thoughts and intents of the heart as well as with people's outward actions. When they realize this, maybe they will perceive the impossibility of ever keeping the law of God, and they will stop trying to work out salvation by an obedience of their own. Show them plainly, lovingly, tenderly, and honestly that *by the works of the Law no flesh will be justified*, for by the law is the knowledge of sin (Romans 3:20).

You know well, my brethren, that people continually try to place a huge stone of error over other people's minds in the form of sacramentalism. To what do they degrade being born again? They make it a ceremony in which drops of water produce marvels. What is feeding upon Christ to these people? It is nothing but eating bread and drinking wine. They put ceremonial absurdities in the place of spiritual truths. They steal the substance and provide mere smoke as a substitute. They do not even give us a shadow as that of the days of Moses, but rather blind the eyes with smoke, and yet multitudes of our fellow creatures are quite content with such emptiness. They suppose that there is some mystic power in outward rites. Tell them that:

> Not all the outward forms of earth,
>    Nor rites that God has given,
> Nor will of man, nor blood, nor birth,
>    Can raise a soul to heaven.[20]

Declare the need of grace and the uselessness of outward show. Teach the spirituality of acceptable worship and the childishness of ritualism. You will have done a good service if you roll away this huge obstruction.

Very frequently the sepulcher of people's souls is closed up by the stone of prejudice. People cannot really find anything wrong with Christ Jesus or His gospel, but they will still persist in stumbling at this stumbling stone. They make up reasons for declining the gospel invitation. They prejudge the revelation of God, and they make up their minds

---
20   This is the first stanza from a hymn by Isaac Watts.

that it is unworthy of their acceptation. They close their eyes, and then are stubborn in their insistence that there is no light. For example, how common is the idea that Christianity is associated with gloominess or depression. In every sphere of life, you will find a number of people who fight without understanding Christianity because they believe it leads to misery of the mind. They quote someone who went insane and then began discussing biblical theories, and another who is full of gloom, yet claims to be a Christian. They imply that Christianity is the science of making long faces, the art of being gloomy. Therefore, people refuse to be soured by "crabby divinity" and decline to imitate the gloomy and depressed Puritans.

That is a big mistake about the Puritans, for there is more than enough evidence to show that they were among the most happy of people with a robust joy. At this present moment, if you want to find a happy group of people, I would advise you to search for them among the true followers of Jesus. It would be a strange thing if having one's sins forgiven would make a person unhappy. It would be a very odd thing if being at peace with God caused a person to be miserable. It would be a very turning of the world upside down if possessing a good hope of heaven would be the source of gloom in the soul. But it is not so.

Brethren, roll away this stone by your continual happiness and obvious cheerfulness, and especially remove it from the minds of young people. Make them see, in the brightness of your countenance, the practical answer to the common false accusation. Convince them that you have an inward joy that they do not understand. Take them to Christ by telling them of the sweetness that you experience in Him.

Many have the idea, too, that true Christianity makes a man unmanly and soft. Some who have professed to be Christians might have given support to this charge by their pretentious manners and lack of common sense. Certain people who claim to be Christians are always dwelling upon the "must nots" of religion, as if godliness was a set of negatives, a garden enclosed with thorns. Making up new commandments is a very fascinating occupation for some people. You must not do this, that, and the other until one feels like a toddler being scolded for everything. I find that ten commandments are more than I can keep without a deal of grace, and I do not intend to pay the slightest regard to any man-made commandments.

Liberty is the genius of our faith, and we do not intend to trade it away for the esteem of modern Pharisees. They say to us, "You shall not laugh on a Sunday. You shall never create a smile in the house of God. You shall go to a church service as though you were going to the whipping post. You shall take care when you preach that you always make your sermon as dull as it can possibly be." We do not reverence these precepts. We honor anything that is of God, but not the sickening decrees of human opinion.

We are men and not slaves. Our manhood is not annihilated by grace. We think, speak, and act for ourselves, and we are not the servants of custom and fashion. We speak our minds even when propriety is shocked and respectability is enraged. I would always give to young men this piece of advice: Act like men, and do not let anyone have to say that your Christianity is weak and without a backbone. Do not always talk in a fake way with every person you speak of as "Dear this," and "Dear that," for this savors of nauseous hypocrisy. Do not whine or turn up your eyes, or pretend to be very devout. Be holy, but not showy. Be true, but not intrusive. Be men, be manly, be Christians – be like Christ. He was the very highest type of man. You never see anything fake or unnatural in Him. He is always Himself – transparent, outspoken, brave, honest, true, and manly. Redeem Christianity from the reproach of pompousness and formalism, and in doing so, roll away one of the stones from the sepulcher.

We know that some people have an idea that Christianity is a mere sentiment or emotion, that it lies in being affected about your dead children and your parents in heaven, in weeping over deathbed scenes. In fact, some see Christianity as excited meetings and the consequent emotions. Some people of the world judge Christianity as consisting only in womanly feelings, thinking that it has no truth, facts, or logic. That is not so. We can give as good a reason for the hope that is in us as though Christianity never brought a tear to our eye and never stirred the emotion of joy within our souls.

I venture to say that the Christian religion is as much based on facts as astronomy or geology. I am talking about indisputable historical facts, and I assert that the doctrines of divine revelation are truths as certain as the principles of mathematics. The gospel reveals certainties, and they are worthy of the contemplation of people of the wisest minds. Our gospel is not mere platitude and baby talk; there is a depth in it that no intellect can fathom. Titanic intellects have found their match in the things of God. The genius of Newton and Locke did not complain of lack of depth in the wondrous truths of God; to them they were waters to swim in. There is room for all the high culture, all the thought, and all the training that this world will ever see. There is room for it, and at its utmost, it will only stand upon the shore of the main ocean of divine truth and cry, "O the depths of the wisdom of the Lord" (Romans 11:33). By intelligently setting forth the great matters of the gospel, let us roll this stone away, for to some it has been a crushing obstruction.

Another stone very commonly lies over the grave among the working class of people, and that is the opinion that the gospel is not for them. I have frequently heard it said by them that it is very proper indeed for ladies and gentlemen and people of money and leisure to be Christians, but it is quite out of the question for someone who has to roll up his sleeves, work hard, and earn a living. They ask, "What do dockyard laborers, cab drivers, and warehouse workers have to do with religion?" Of all the strange prejudices in existence, this is one of the strangest, because from time immemorial it has been the boast of the gospel that *the poor have the gospel preached to them* (Matthew 11:5). If there is one group of people to whom the gospel is more joyful tidings than to any other, it is to those who labor and are heavy laden (Matthew 11:28).

Dear friends, if you only have a little in this life, that is even more reason why you should seek the unlimited treasures of the life to come. If you have much trouble and sorrow here, that is more reason why you should seek Christ to be the balm of all your wounds and the healing medicine of all your cares. Christianity gained its apostles from the working classes, and from that same source it has gathered countless martyrs. Although the Lord has had a remnant in the upper class, it remains true that not many mighty and noble people are called (1 Corinthians 1:26). The great majority of Christian discipleship has been taken from among the poor and the working class of people.

Besides, Christ is the people's Christ. What a wonderful sentence that is from the Psalms: *I have exalted one chosen from the people* (Psalm 89:19). Jesus is the people's man by birth, by education, and by sympathy. He was ordained of God to be a leader and commander for the people. Jesus Christ is just such a friend as the people need. Tell the people so, especially you who belong to them and know it. Make your houses preaching places to your fellow workers, and make your conduct a constant sermon about adapting the gospel of Jesus Christ to their needs. So much for the stone of prejudice, but I must move on.

Frequently over the graves of spiritually dead persons, there lies a stone of loneliness. They feel as if no one cares for their soul. I have known that to happen in this church, in our own London Metropolitan Tabernacle. People have attended for months and nobody has spoken to them because they were strangers. Therefore, the gospel did not enter into their hearts because they said, "The church of God does not care for us; we are unknown and unvalued." Half a word from some kind Christian sitting near them has often been the means of melting them down, and the very next sermon they have heard has been, in God's hands, the means of bringing them to Christ.

A person can lose himself in this city more completely than he could in the desert of Sahara. You can get away into one of our streets, and even work in one of our factories, and nobody will interest himself about you. While a few people might pry into their neighbor's affairs, even fewer have any sympathy for their neighbor's griefs. Hearts may be breaking around us while we are as merry as May. Children of God, I urge you in the name of the life-giving Savior, never let this stone lie two Sundays together over the grave of a single person who attends this church, but prove to those who sit with you here that you have a loving care for their souls.

Another stone that can be rolled away is that of degradation. Some people take themselves into the ditch by their sins. They break the rules of society, they become dangerous, and in time they are treated as outcasts. When a person feels himself banned, how little hope there is of raising him! Many sink themselves to poverty by their sins and excesses, and thousands degrade themselves by abominable drunkenness. The Christian church does well when it uses its utmost power to deliver the drunkard from his besetting sin. Abstinence from alcohol will not take the place of godliness, but it might put people in the way of gospel influences.

God forbid that we should stop short in any reforms, for we must completely roll away the stone from the grave, and we must not let any stone remain. Many people have first been delivered from the habit of intoxication, and then their ears have been opened to listen to the truth as it is in Jesus. The poor prostitute, too, when Christian love has followed her and spoken to her about our Father who is in heaven and who desires the wandering to return to Him, how often have her feelings of degradation been overcome, and she has fled to Christ for mercy?

Brethren, none are outcasts to us. If the world says to the fallen, "Get out of here; you are not good enough for us," let the church of God open her door and invite the outcasts in. The church is the true hospital for those sick in sin, among whom Jesus delights to work. It is our glory to restore those whom the world calls lepers and contemptuously drives away. Come here, you chief of sinners, for Jesus waits to receive you. Do not delay, for He came to save you and those like you. The Pharisees drive you away, but *this man receives sinners and eats with them* (Luke 15:2).

We will mention one more stone, and that is the stone of despair. Some people are not only spiritually dead, but they are buried very deep in despair. They have signed their own death warrants, even though the Lord has not yet written them out. You people of God, keep a watchful eye out for those who think they are beyond all hope, and when you meet with them, argue the point with them. Tell them that you were once in the same situation as they are, and show them what grace did for you. Point them to the promises of God that are so suitable to their condition. Above all, tell them of the precious Savior, who does not put out the smoldering wick (Matthew 12:20), and who is able to save to the uttermost those who *draw near to God through Him* (Hebrews 7:25). You will have done a good thing if you roll away the stone of despair. I exhort you, dear fellow laborers in Christ, you who are saved, do all that you can to take away every one of these hinderances from the souls of sinners, and then pray to the Lord to speak the life-giving word.

**Second, there are some things that we can do for people after they have been made alive in Christ.**

After a person is converted, he labors under many disadvantages, and Christian love should help him. When lambs are born, the shepherd takes care of them. Christ tells us to feed His lambs (John 21:15). When plants are put into the ground, they must be watered. It is not enough that the child is born, but he needs a mother's care. *Take this child away and nurse him for me and I will give you your wages* (Exodus 2:9) is God's word to His people whenever a new convert is born into His family. Lazarus is alive, but he is weighed down with graveclothes. It is the duty of his friends to loose him and let him go.

New converts need to be set free for the sake of their own comfort. It was a very uncomfortable thing for Lazarus to be tied up in his burial cloths. For his own comfort they must be taken off. When a person is saved, he might not grasp all that is involved in salvation. He thinks, "I am a Christian, but I can fall from grace." Unwrap that cloth at once and let him know that the Lord does not cast away His people whom He foreknew (Romans 11:2). He thinks that he is forgiven, but he also thinks that some sin might still remain upon him. Unwind that cloth and let him know that *the blood of Jesus His Son cleanses us from all sin* (1 John 1:7). Maybe when he feels strife within himself he imagines that he is not really a child of God. Tear off that bandage and tell him that all children of God experience inward strife and feel a battle raging between life and death within their souls. You will find that new converts tend to be the victims of doubts and fears, worrying themselves about this and that. You who are instructed in the faith must make a sincere effort to unbind them and let them go.

New converts also need to be set free for the sake of their own freedom. Lazarus might as well be in the grave as bound in burial cloths. People can be converted and yet be far from enjoying the full liberty of the children of God. Maybe the saved one is chained by bad habits, but he does not know that they are bad; tell him gently, but let him know that these things are not consistent with a Christian life. I know some real Christians who are going around with remnants of their graveclothes upon them, and they appear very improper. Those graveclothes cling to all of us, more or less. I suppose that the unbinding will need to be continued until we enter heaven, but let us help our brethren in this by example and by precept. Let us take away from them that which hinders them from the liberty of holiness.

Moreover, Lazarus needed to be unbound for the sake of fellowship. He could not talk with Mary and Martha yet, for he had a cloth around his head. He could hardly move or speak. So many of our dear converts do not like to join the church yet. They say they are not perfect. Poor souls; if they were perfect, we would not want them in our churches. Since none of us are perfect, they would be out of place if they joined with us. They plead that they are not fit to come, imagining that something more is needed beyond believing in Christ – as if that which Jesus laid down as the gospel of salvation was not also a sufficient basis for fellowship with saints on earth. Still, the timid hold back and do not like to tell others what the Lord has done for them. Encourage them and compel them to come in. Do not let them wander in solitude, but introduce them to the fellowship of the saints.

We have known cases in which liberty was needed to enable new converts to bear testimony. Lazarus could not even say, "I live, and blessed be the name of God," for the cloth was around his head. He had to be unbound so that he could tell others what God had done. Oh, what pleasant testimonies the church might have if saints were only encouraged to deliver them, but there are some who disapprove and hinder, and the moment a young Christian talks about Christ, because he does not speak exactly according to traditional doctrine, they try to silence him. Let it never be so among us. Let us encourage the infant converts to cry so that soon they will learn to speak. Let us encourage them to babble, for perhaps before long they will correctly speak the language of the kingdom.

Just as their testimonies are needed, so their service is needed. Paul was converted on the road to Damascus, but he did not know what God intended to do with him, and he was not ready for God to use until Ananias had instructed him (Acts 9:6). It was the same with Apollos. He was a true Christian, but he needed further teaching (Acts 18:26). He needed to be unbound and let go, and Aquilla and Priscilla became the instruments of doing so. There was the eunuch on his way to Ethiopia; he needed to learn more about the Scriptures, to have the meaning of the prophet Isaiah opened up to him, and to be baptized on profession of his faith in Christ (Acts 8:26-40).

Do not allow any of God's dear living ones to be waiting bound up and captive because we are so devoid of brotherly love that we will not do for them the needful duties of heavenly love and kindness. May the Lord help us, brethren, to be earnest about this.

After Lazarus was unbound, we read that he sat at the table with Jesus. He needed to be unbound so that he could enjoy communion with Christ. The trembling convert thinks himself not yet permitted to lay hold upon the nearer, dearer, and sweeter joys that surround the person of Christ. He thinks that these are reserved for old, mature saints, and that they are for people who have fought the good fight and almost finished their course (1 Timothy 4:7); but he certainly errs and deprives himself of joy.

The songs of Zion are for the early morning as well as for the shades of evening. Go and tell young Christians so. Encourage them to commune with Jesus. Tell them that He loves all His people with an equal love and is ready to make Himself known to them as He does not unto the world (John 14:22). In this aspect you will unbind them and let them go.

I will finish with two questions that I want to put very plainly. The first is this: Dear brethren, I have told you what can be done for sinners before conversion. I have told you what can be done for them afterward. I want to ask how many of you are doing either one? I will not take my pen and make a list of the diligent among you, but I will ask each person's conscience to act as a scribe and to write down your name if you are really serving Christ. Beloved, it does no good to merely talk about our duty. We must be daily and constantly doing it. Time is gliding away, people are dying, hell is filling, and Christ's name is being dishonored. There are only twelve hours in the day; are we walking while we have the light (John 12:35), and are we working for God while we have the opportunity?

If every one of us will give an honest answer to that question, it will do us good, even if we have to confess that we have been lazy. Asking ourselves that question might lead to shame, and then to confession, to prayer, and to a renovation of life, for if we are indeed the Lord's, let us live while we live. Much of professing Christian life nowadays is something to be ashamed of. It is cold, weak, narrow, and fainthearted. I see passion and devotion everywhere except among Christians. I see drive and push and vigor in business. I see the world encircled so that people can send the messages of commerce with lightning speed, while the message of the gospel lags behind. I see the mountains cut out, and it may be next that the sea's deep bed may be tunneled. People do anything for the things of this world, but how little will they do for the things of heaven. May God revive us so that we will be a living, earnest people!

The other question is this: How far is the Lord Jesus working in our families and among our acquaintances in the matter of raising the spiritually dead? Are your children saved yet? Are your employees regenerated yet? Are your brothers and sisters saved yet? Has God given new life to your husbands and wives? Come, let us ask this question to others, too. The angel asked Lot, "Do you have any others here?" (Genesis 19:12). That is a very serious question.

Oh, that God would grant that we would be like Noah, who had all his sons, and his sons' wives, and his own wife in the ark with him. May we never stop praying until it is so. If there is even one unconverted person who is linked with us in any way, let us pray day and night until that soul is saved, and then let us go after the neighborhood in which we dwell and the streets where we reside. May God help this great city, this perishing city, and visit it in mercy.

I believe He will, if He finds us willing to do the work of rolling away the stone and being equally willing to unloose the burial cloths. God will not send children to us if we cannot nurse them. He will not send lambs to us if we will not shepherd them. God is not so unkind to newborn souls as to send them among a people who do not care for them. He will make us travail in birth before children will be born to God here, because soul travail is the means by which love works in us toward them so that we are taught to handle them affectionately, cherish them carefully, and bring them up for the Lord.

O beloved Christians over whom Christ rejoices, I ask you to serve the Lord Jesus with diligence in this divine service of doing good to the sons of men.

God bless you, beloved, for Christ's sake. Amen.

## Chapter 10

# Unbinding Lazarus

*When He had said these things, He cried out with a loud voice, "Lazarus, come forth." The man who had died came forth, bound hand and foot with wrappings, and his face was wrapped around with a cloth. Jesus said to them, "Unbind him, and let him go." (John 11:43-44)*

Our Lord Jesus stands alone as a worker in many things. No one else can unite His voice with the command that says, *Lazarus, come forth*. Yet in certain points of the gracious work of God, the Master joins His servants with Him, so that when Lazarus has come forth, He says to them, *Unbind him, and let him go*. In raising the dead, Jesus is alone, and in this He is majestic and divine. In setting free those who are bound, He joins with His disciples, yet still remains majestic.

His more prominent feature, though, is His condescension – He lowers Himself to be with us. How exceedingly kind it is of our Lord Jesus to allow His disciples to do some little thing in connection with His great deeds so that they can be workers together with Him (2 Corinthians 6:1). As often as possible, our Lord joined His disciples with Himself. Of course, they could not help Him in presenting an atoning sacrifice, but it was their honor that they had said, *Let us also go, so that we may die with Him* (John 11:16), and that in their love they resolved to go with Him to prison and to death.

Our Lord understood the fickleness of their character, yet He knew that they were sincere in their desire to be associated with Him in every part of His life – whatever it might be. When He later rode into Jerusalem in triumph, He alone was honored with cheers of "Hosanna," but He sent two of His disciples to bring the donkey on which He rode. They cast their garments upon the colt and set Jesus upon it, and as He went, they spread their clothes in the way. Thus, they contributed to His lowly splendor and shared in the exultation of the royal day.

A little later, when Jesus wanted to keep the feast, He specifically stated that He wanted to keep it with them, for He said, *I have earnestly desired to eat this Passover with you before I suffer* (Luke 22:15). He sent Peter and John to prepare for that Passover, He directed them to the large furnished upper room, and He told them to get things ready. They were allowed to do anything that they could do.

Their Lord was willing to have led them even further, but through weakness they stopped short. In the garden He told them to watch with Him on that dreadful night, and He sought sympathy from them.

> Backward and forward thrice He ran,
> As if He sought some help from man.[21]

He cried in sorrowful disappointment, Could you *not keep watch with Me for one hour?* (Matthew 26:40). Ah, no! They could go to the edge of the abyss with Him, but they could not descend into its depths. He must tread the winepress alone, and of the people there must be none with Him (Isaiah 63:3); yet as far as they could go, He did not scorn their dear society. He allowed them to drink of His cup and to be baptized with His baptism according to their capacity, and if their fellowship with Him in His sufferings went no further, it was not because He warned them to stay away, but because they did not have the strength to follow. According to His own judgment, they were intimately associated with Him, for He said to them, *You are those who have stood by Me in My trials* (Luke 22:28).

Beloved, our Jesus Christ still delights for us to associate with Him as far as our weakness and foolishness will permit. In His present work of

---

[21] This is from a hymn by Joseph Hart that begins with "Come, all ye chosen saints of God."

bringing sinners to Himself, He considers it a part of His reward that we would be laborers together with Him. He sees the travail of His soul in His working people, as well as in the sinners whom they bring to Him. Thus, He has a double reward, and He is as much glorified in the love, compassion, and zeal of His servants as in the harvest that they reap.

Just as a father smiles to see his little children imitating him and trying to assist him in his work, so Jesus is pleased to see our lowly efforts to honor Him. It is His joy to see the eyes that He has opened weeping with Him over the unrepentant. It is His joy to hear the tongue that He has loosed speaking in prayer and in proclaiming the gospel. Yes, it brings Him joy to see any whom He has restored and healed who are now busy as members of righteousness in His service.

Jesus is glad to save sinners by any means, but He is most of all glad to save them by the means of those who are already saved. Thus He blesses the prodigal sons and the servants of the household at the same time. He gives salvation to the lost, and upon His own called and chosen ones He puts the honor of being used for the greatest purposes under heaven. It is more honorable to save a soul from death than to rule an empire. All the saints can have such honor.

The main subject of this chapter is our association with Christ in pious labor, but we must consider other themes that lead up to it. First, I would call your attention to a memorable miracle that was wrought by our Lord in the burying place at Bethany. Second, I want to look at a remarkable spectacle, for in Lazarus we see a living man wearing the garments of the dead. Third, we will learn something from a timely assistance, which the friends around the grave gave to the risen man after the Lord had said, *Unbind him, and let him go.* Then, by way of conclusion, we will observe a practical hint that this whole subject gives to those who are willing to hear what Christ their Lord will speak to them. Oh, that the Spirit of God may make us quick of understanding to perceive the mind of the Lord, and then diligent of heart to carry out His will! *Come, O blessed Spirit, and help Your servant at this hour!*

**First, then, this chapter records a memorable miracle.**
Maybe that writer is correct who says that the raising of Lazarus is the most remarkable of all our Lord's mighty works. We cannot measure

miracles, for they are all displays of the infinite, but in some respects the raising of Lazarus stands at the head of the wonderful series of miracles with which our Lord astonished and instructed the people. Yet I am not in error when I state that it is a type of what the Lord Jesus is constantly doing at this hour in the realm of mind and spirit. Did He raise the naturally dead? He still raises the spiritually dead. Did He bring back a body from corruption? He still delivers people from loathsome sins. The life-giving miracle of grace is as truly astounding as the life-giving miracle of power. As this was in some respects a more remarkable resurrection than the raising of Jairus's daughter, or of the young man at the gate of Nain, so there are certain conversions and regenerations that seem more astonishing than others to the observing mind.

I notice the memorableness of this miracle in the subject of it, because the man had been dead four days. To give life to one about whom his own sister said, *Lord, by this time there will be a stench* (John 11:39), was a deed filled with divine power. Corruption had set in, but He who is the resurrection and the life stopped and reversed the process. The sisters had probably perceived the traces of decay upon the body of their beloved brother before they buried him, for it is likely that they delayed the funeral as long as possible under an undefined hope that perhaps their Lord would appear upon the scene. In that warm climate, the ravages of decay are extremely rapid, and before many hours the loving sisters were compelled to admit, as Abraham had done before them (Genesis 23:4), that they must bury their dead out of their sight. It was their full conviction that the terrible consuming of corruption had begun. What then can be done?

When someone has very recently died, and every vein and artery is in its place and every separate organ is still perfect, it might seem possible for the life-blood to flow again. It somewhat resembles an engine that was just recently in full action, and although it is now motionless, the valves, wheels, and belts are still there. Simply start it up again, reapply the moving force, and the machinery will quickly begin to work. However, when corruption comes, every valve is displaced, every wheel is broken, every belt is severed, and the very metal itself is eaten away. What can be done now? Certainly it would be an easier task to make a completely new person out of the earth than to take this poor corrupted corpse that has turned to worms' meat and make it live again. This was the marvelous miracle of divine power that our glorious Lord performed upon His friend Lazarus.

There are some men who are represented by this situation. Not only are they devoid of all spiritual life, but corruption has set in. Their character has become abhorrent, their language is filthy, and their attitude is terrible. The pure mind desires to have them put out of sight, for they cannot be endured in any decent society. They are so far gone from original righteousness as to be an offense to all, and it does not seem possible that they could ever be restored to purity, honesty, or hope. When the Lord in infinite compassion comes to deal with them and gives them life, then even the most skeptical must confess, *This is the finger of God* (Exodus 8:19). What else can it be? Such a profane sinner became a believer! Such a blasphemer became a man of prayer! Such a proud, conceited babbler received the kingdom as a little child! Surely God Himself must have worked this wonder!

Now is fulfilled the word of the Lord by Ezekiel: *You will know that I am the* LORD, *when I have opened your graves and caused you to come up out of your graves, My people* (Ezekiel 37:13). We thank our God that He gives life to the dry bones, whose hope was lost. However far gone a person may be, he cannot be beyond the reach of the Lord's right arm of mighty mercy. The Lord can change the vilest of the vile into the most holy of the holy! Blessed be His name, we have seen Him do this, and therefore we have encouraging hope for the worst men and women!

The next notable point about this miracle is the clear human weakness of its worker. He who had to deal with this dead man was Himself a man. I do not know of any passage of Scripture wherein the manhood of Christ is more frequently manifested than in this narrative. The Godhead is, of course, eminently noticeable in the resurrection of Lazarus, but the Lord seemed as if He deliberately at the same time set His humanity to the front. According to the forty-seventh verse, the Pharisees said, *What are we doing? For this man is performing many signs.* They are to be blamed for denying His Godhead, but not for dwelling upon His manhood, for every part of this exceptional scene before us made it obvious.

When our Lord had seen Mary's tears, we read that *He was deeply moved in spirit and was troubled* (John 11:33). Thus He showed the sorrows and the sympathies of a man. We cannot forget those memorable words, *Jesus wept* (John 11:35). Who except a person would weep? Weeping is a human characteristic. Jesus never seems to be more completely bone of our bone and flesh of our flesh than when He weeps.

Next, our Lord asked a question: *Where have you laid him?* (John 11:34). He veils His omniscience. As a man, He seeks information: where is the body of His dear departed friend? Even as Mary later said about Jesus, *Tell me where you have laid Him* (John 20:15), so the Lord Jesus asked for information as someone who did not know. As if to show His manhood even more fully, when they told Him where Lazarus was buried, He went that way. He did not need to go. He could have spoken a word where He was, and the dead would have risen. Could He not just as easily have performed the miracle from a distance as He could have done by being nearby?

Being man, *Jesus, again being deeply moved within, came to the tomb* (John 11:38). When He reached the spot, He saw a cave whose mouth was closed by a huge stone, and He sought human assistance. He cried, *Remove the stone* (John 11:39). Certainly He who could raise the dead could have rolled away the stone by speaking a word! Yet, as if needing help from those around Him, the man Christ Jesus reminded us again of Mary at His own tomb, saying, *Who will roll away the stone for us?* (Mark 16:3).

With that done, our Lord lifted up His eyes to heaven and addressed the Father in prayer mingled with thanksgiving. How like a man is all this! He takes the petitioner's place. He speaks with God as a man speaks with his friend (Exodus 33:11), but still as a man. Did not this humble revelation of the manhood make the miracle all the more remarkable? The time came when the flame of the Godhead flashed forth from the unconsumed bush of the manhood. The voice of Him who wept was heard in the chambers of death's shadow, and out came the soul of Lazarus to live again in the body. *The weakness of God* (1 Corinthians 1:25) proved itself to be stronger than death and mightier than the grave.

It is a parable of our own situation as workers for Christ. Sometimes we see the human side of the gospel, and we wonder whether it can do many mighty works. When we tell the story, we fear that it will seem repetitious to the people. We wonder how it can be that truth so simple, so familiar, and so common would have any special power about it. Yet it is so. Out of the foolishness of preaching, the wisdom of God shines forth (1 Corinthians 1:21). The glory of the eternal God is seen in that gospel that we preach in much trembling and weakness. Let us therefore glory in our infirmity (2 Corinthians 12:9) because the power of God does all the more evidently rest upon us. Let us not despise our *day of small things* (Zechariah 4:10) nor be dismayed because we are obviously so weak. This work is not for our honor, but for the glory of God, and any circumstance that tends to make that glory more evident is to be rejoiced in.

Let us consider for a few moments the active cause of this resurrection. Nothing was used by our Lord but His own word of power. Jesus cried with a loud voice, *Lazarus, come forth* (John 11:43). He simply repeated the dead man's name and added two commanding words. This was simple enough. Dear friends, a miracle seems all the greater when the means used are apparently feeble and not well adapted to the working of such a great result.

It is the same way in the salvation of men. It is marvelous that such poor preaching should convert such great sinners. Many are turned unto the Lord by the simplest, plainest, and most unadorned preaching of the gospel. They may not hear much, but the little that they hear is from the lips of Jesus. Many converts find Christ by a single short sentence. The divine life is carried into their hearts upon the wings of a brief text. The preacher had no eloquence, and he made no attempt at it, but the Holy Spirit spoke through him with a power that eloquence could not rival. The Lord told the dry bones to live, and they came to life (Ezekiel 37).

I delight to preach my Master's gospel in the plainest terms. I would speak even more simply if I could. I would borrow the language of Daniel concerning Belshazzar's robe of scarlet and his chain of gold, and I would say to eloquence, *Keep your gifts for yourself or give your rewards to someone else* (Daniel 5:17). The power to awaken the dead does not lie in the wisdom of words, but in the Spirit of the living God (1 Corinthians 2:4). The voice is Christ's voice, and the word is the word of Him who is the resurrection and the life, and therefore people are made alive by it. Let us rejoice that it is not needful for us to become orators in order for the Lord Jesus to speak through us. Simply let the Spirit of God rest upon us, and we will be endowed with power from on high (Luke 24:49) so that even the spiritually dead will hear the voice of the Son of God through us, and they who hear will live.

The result of the Lord's working must not be missed, for it is a main element of wonder in this miracle. Lazarus did come forth, and He did so immediately. The thunder of Christ's voice was attended by the lightning of His divine power, and immediately life flashed into Lazarus, and he came forth. Bound as he was, the power that had enabled him to live enabled him to shuffle forth from the ledge of rock upon which he lay, and there he stood with nothing of death about him but his graveclothes. He left the stale air of the sepulcher and returned to know once more the things that are done under the sun, and it happened quickly.

It is one of the great glories of the gospel that it does not require weeks or months for people to be given life and to make new creations of them; salvation can come to them at once. The person who stepped into this church this morning immersed in rebellion against his God, and apparently impervious to divine truth, may nevertheless go down those steps with his sins forgiven and with a new spirit imparted to him, in the strength of which he will begin to live unto God as he never lived before. Do you speak of a nation being born at once, as if it were impossible (Isaiah 66:8)? It is possible with God. The Divine Power can send a flash of life all around the world at any instant to give life to multitudes of His chosen. We are dealing now with God, not with men.

Man must have time to prepare his machinery and get it into working order, but it is not so with the Lord. We, on our part, must seek after a preacher and find a place for him where the people can meet to hear; but when the Lord Jesus works, the action is done immediately, with or without the preacher, and inside or outside the place of assembly! If we had to feed five thousand, we would need to grind the wheat at the mill and bake the bread in the oven, and then we would be a long time in delivering the loaves in baskets; but the Master takes the barley cakes and breaks them, and as He breaks them, the food is multiplied. Then He handles the fish, and it seems as if a multitude of fish had been in His hands instead of *a few small fish* (Matthew 15:34). Behold! The vast multitude receives nourishment from the little supply that has been so abundantly increased.

Trust in God, my brethren. In all your work of love, trust in the unseen power that stood behind the manhood of Christ, and that still stands behind the simple gospel that we preach. The everlasting Word may seem to be weak and feeble. It might groan and weep and seem as if it could do no more, but it can raise the dead, and raise them at once. You can be sure of this.

The effect that this miracle produced upon those who saw it was very remarkable, for many believed in the Lord Jesus. Besides this, the miracle of raising Lazarus was so unquestioned and unquestionable a fact that it brought the Pharisees to a point that they resolved to make an end of Christ. They had grumbled and muttered at His earlier miracles, but this one had struck such a blow that in their wrath they determined that He should die. No doubt this miracle was the immediate cause of the crucifixion of Jesus. It marked a point of decision when people must either believe in Christ or become His deadly foes.

Oh, brethren, if the Lord is with us, we will see multitudes believing through Jesus. If the rage of the enemy becomes more intense because of this, let us not fear it, for there will come a last decisive struggle, and it might be brought on by some amazing display of the divine power in the conversion of the chief of sinners. Let us hope so. Let us not be afraid that Armageddon should be fought, for it will end in victory. *You will see greater things than these* (John 1:50).

**Second, I ask you to observe a remarkable spectacle.**
A notable miracle was unquestionably performed, but it required a finishing touch. The man was completely raised to life, but was not completely freed. Here is a living man in the garments of death. That cloth around his head and other graveclothes were completely consistent with death, but they were very much out of place when Lazarus began to live again. It is a dismal sight to see a living man wearing his burial clothes, but hundreds of times we have seen in this church people made alive by divine grace who still had their graveclothes upon them. Such was their condition that unless you observed carefully, you would think they were still dead, yet within them the lamp of heavenly life was

burning. Some said, "He is dead; look at his garments," but the more spiritual people cried, "He is not dead, but these graveclothes must be loosed." It is a remarkable spectacle – a living man restricted with the garments of death!

Moreover, he was a moving man bound hand and foot. I do not know how he moved. Some of the old writers thought that he glided, as it were, through the air, and that this was part of the miracle. I think he may have been so bound that although he could not freely walk, he could shuffle along like a man in a sack. I know that I have seen souls bound and yet moving. They were moving intensely in one direction, yet were not capable of moving an inch in another.

Have you not seen someone so truly alive that he wept, mourned, and groaned over sin, yet he could not believe in Christ, but seemed bound hand and foot as to faith? I have seen him determined to give up his sin and crush a bad habit under his foot, yet he could not lay hold on a promise or receive a hope. Lazarus was free enough in one way, for he came out of the tomb, but the blinding cloth was around his head. This is how it is with many awakened sinners, for when you try to show them some encouraging truth, they cannot see it.

This was a repulsive sight, but captivating. Mary and Martha must have been delighted to see their brother, even though he was wrapped in graveclothes. He stunned the crowd, yet they were drawn to him. A man fresh from the sepulcher dressed in graveclothes is a sight that most people would want to avoid, but such a man was Lazarus; yet people would travel around the world to see a man restored from death, and such a man was Lazarus.

Mary and Martha felt their hearts dancing within them because their dear brother was alive. Notwithstanding the repulsiveness of the spectacle, it must have pleased them beyond anything they had seen except the Lord Himself. We, too, may have come near to a poor sinner; it was enough to frighten anybody to hear his groans and to see his weeping, yet he was so dear to every true heart that we loved to be with him. I have sometimes spoken with brokenhearted sinners, and they have pretty nearly broken my heart; yet after they had left the room, I wished I could see a thousand like them. Poor creatures – they fill us with sorrow, yet flood us with joy.

This was a man who was strong, yet helpless. He was strong enough to come forth from his grave, yet he could not take the cloth away from his own head, for his hands were bound. He could not go to his house, for his feet were wrapped. Unless some kind hand unbound him, he would remain a living mummy. He had enough strength to leave the grave, but he could not be released from his graveclothes.

In the same way, we have seen men who were strong, for the Spirit of God has been in them and has moved them mightily. They have been passionately in earnest, even to the point of agony, yet the newborn life has been so weak in other ways that they seemed to have been mere infants in swaddling clothes. They have not been able to enjoy the liberty of Christ, nor enter into communion with Christ, nor work for Christ. They have been bound hand and foot; work and progress have both been beyond them.

This seems to be a strange result of a miracle. The bands of death were loosed, but not the bands of linen. Motion was given, but not movement of hand or foot. Strength was bestowed upon him, but not the power to undress himself. Such anomalies are common in the world of grace.

**This brings us to consider a timely assistance that we are called upon to give.**
O for wisdom to learn our duty, and grace to do it at once. Let us consider what these things are that often bind newly converted sinners. Some of them are blindfolded by the cloth around their head. They are very ignorant, sadly lacking in spiritual wisdom, and the eye of faith is darkened. Yet the eye is there, and Christ has opened it. It is the business of the servant of God to remove the cloth that bandages it. We can do so by teaching the truth, explaining it, and clearing up difficulties. This is a simple thing to do, and it is very necessary. Now that they have life, we will teach them its purpose. Besides that, they are bound hand and foot, so are not able to act. We can show them how to work for Jesus.

Sometimes these bands are those of sorrow, for they are in dreadful fear about the past. We must unbind them by showing them that the past is blotted out. They are wrapped about by many yards of doubt, mistrust, anguish, and remorse. Unbind them, and let them go.

Another hindrance is the band of fear. "Oh," says the poor soul, "I am such a sinner that God must punish me for my sin." Tell him about the great doctrine of substitution. Unwrap this cloth by the assurance that Jesus took our sin, and that *by His scourging we are healed* (Isaiah 53:5). It is wonderful what liberty comes by that precious truth when it is well understood. The repentant soul fears that Jesus will refuse his prayer. Assure him that Jesus will certainly not cast out any who come to Him (John 6:37). Let fear be taken from the soul by the promises of Scripture, by our testimony to their truth, and by the Spirit bearing witness to the doctrine that we try to proclaim.

People are very often bound with the graveclothes of prejudice. They used to think certain things before conversion, and they are very apt to carry their dead thoughts into their new life. Go and tell them that things are not what they seem. *The old things passed away; behold, new things have come* (2 Corinthians 5:17). God is overlooking their days of ignorance (Acts 17:30), but now they must change their minds about everything and no longer judge according to the sight of the eyes and the hearing of the ears.

Some of them are bound with the graveclothes of sinful habits. It is a noble work to help a drunkard remove the detestable bands that prevent him from making the slightest progress toward better things. Let us tear off every band from ourselves so that we can more easily help others to be free. The bonds of evil habits can still remain upon people who have received the divine life – until those habits are pointed out to them and the sinfulness of them is shown, and so they are helped by understanding, prayer, and example to be free.

Who among us would want Lazarus to continue wearing his burial clothes? Who would want to see a regenerated person fall into sinful habits? When the Lord gives life, the main point of the business is secured, and then we can come in to loose every bond that would restrict and hinder the free action of the divine life.

But why are these cloths left? Why did not the miracle that raised Lazarus also loosen his graveclothes? I answer that it is because our Lord Jesus is always prudent regarding miracles. There are many false wonders, but true miracles are few and far between. In the Church of Rome, such miracles that they claim are usually an abundant waste of power. When St. Swithin supposedly made it rain for forty days so that his corpse would not be carried into the church, it was much ado about very little. When St. Denis supposedly walked a thousand miles carrying his head in his hands, one is inclined to ask why he could not have journeyed just as well if he had set it on his neck. When another saint supposedly crossed the sea on a tablecloth, would it not have been an improvement if he had borrowed a boat? Rome can afford to be free with her counterfeit coins.

The Lord Jesus never works a miracle unless there is an object to be gained that could not be obtained in any other way. When the Enemy said, *Command that these stones become bread* (Matthew 4:3), our Lord refused, for it was not a proper occasion for a miracle. Lazarus cannot be raised out of the grave except by a miracle, but he can be unbound without a miracle, and therefore human hands must do it. If there is anything in the kingdom of God that we can do ourselves, it is foolish to say, "May the Lord do it," for He will do nothing of the kind. If you can do it, you will do it. If you refuse to do it, you will be neglectful of your duty.

I suppose that those graveclothes were left on Lazarus so that those who came to unbind him could be sure that he was the same man who died. Some of them may have said, "This is Lazarus, for these are the graveclothes that we wrapped around him. There is no deceit here. This is the very same man who was laid out and prepared by us for burial." "I remember putting in that stitch," someone says. "I remember that stain in the linen," declares another.

From coming so near to Lazarus, they would be equally well assured that he was really alive! They saw his living flesh rising as each strip of cloth was removed. They observed his breathing and the flush that reddened his cheeks. For some such reason our Lord allows the awakened sinner to remain in a measure of bondage so that we can know that the person is the same one who was really dead in trespasses and sins. He was no pretend sinner, for the traces of his sins are still upon him. You can see by what he says that his training was not the best. The remnants of the old nature show what manner of man he used to be. Every now and then the smell of the sepulcher meets your nose. The mold of the grave has stained his graveclothes. His death was true, and was not a mere imitation of death.

So, too, we know that he is alive, for we hear his sighs and cries, and we understand that his experience is that of a living child of God. Those desires, that searching of heart, and that longing to be thoroughly right with God – we know what these things mean. It is a big help to us in discerning spirits and in being assured of the work of God upon any person for us to come into living contact with those imperfections that it is to be our privilege to remove under the guidance of the Holy Spirit.

I still think that the main purpose was so these disciples could enter into rare fellowship with Christ. They could each say, not proudly but still joyfully, "Our Lord raised Lazarus, and I was there and helped to unbind him from his graveclothes." Maybe Martha could later say, "I took the napkin from my brother's dear face." Maybe Mary could add, "I helped to unbind his hands." It is very precious to hope that we have done anything to cheer, teach, or sanctify a soul. There can be no praise for us in this, but there can be much comfort for us concerning this.

Brothers and sisters, will you not share in this dear delight? Will you not seek the lost sheep (Luke 15:3-7)? Will you not sweep the house for the lost money (Luke 15:8-10)? Will you not at the very least help with the feast for the long-lost son (Luke 15:11-32)? This, you see, gives you such an interest in a saved person. Those who are very observant tell us that those whom we serve may forget us, but those who serve us are firmly bound to us by their deed. You can do many kind things for people who will be entirely ungrateful, but those who have done the kind act do not forget.

When the Lord Jesus has us help others, it is partly so that they will love us for what we have done, but it is even more so that we will love them because we have helped them. Is there any love like the love of a mother to her child? Is it not the strongest affection on earth? Why does a mother love her child? Did the little child ever provide even a penny's worth of service to the mother? Certainly not. It is the mother who does everything for the child. In the same way, the Lord binds us to the new converts in love by allowing us to help them. The church is made entirely of one piece and is woven together all throughout by the workmanship of love. O you who are lacking love, it is evident that you do not labor with a pure desire to benefit others, for if you did, you would be filled with affection for them.

Before we leave this point of timely assistance, let us ask why we should remove these graveclothes. It is enough to say that the Lord has told us to do so. He commands us to *unbind him, and let him go.* He tells us to comfort the fainthearted and help the weak (1 Thessalonians 5:14). If He commands it, we do not need any other reason. I hope, my dear friends, that you will get to work at once, for the King's business requires haste (1 Samuel 21:8), and we are traitors if we delay.

We should also do this because it is very possible that we helped to bind those graveclothes upon our friend. Some of the people who were at Bethany that day had assisted in the burial of Lazarus, and surely the ones who helped to bind Lazarus should also help to unbind him. Many Christians before their conversions have helped to make sinners worse by their examples, and possibly after their conversions they might have assisted in binding new converts in the bonds of doubt and sorrow by their indifference and lack of zeal. In any case, you might have said of many people, "He will never be saved!" In doing so, you have wrapped him in graveclothes. The Lord never told you to do that, but you did it on your own; and now that He tells you to remove those graveclothes, will you not be quick to do so?

I remember when somebody lent a hand to take the graveclothes off me, and therefore I desire to help take the graveclothes off others. If we cannot repay what we owe to the precise individual who did good to us, we can at least repay it by working for the general benefit of seekers. "There," said a benevolent man as he gave help to a poor man, "take that money, and when you can pay it back, give it to the next person you meet who is in the same situation as yourself, and tell him he is to pay it to another destitute person as soon as he can afford it. In this way, my money will go traveling on for many days."

That is what our Lord does. He sends someone to loose my bonds. Then I am helped to set another free, and he releases a third, and so on to the end of the world. God grant that we may not be negligent in this heavenly service.

### Lastly, here is a practical hint.

If the Lord Jesus Christ used the disciples to relieve Lazarus of his graveclothes, do you not think He would use us if we were ready for such work? Observe Saul, now known as the apostle Paul: the Lord Jesus has struck him down, but the lowly Ananias must visit him and baptize him so that he can receive his sight. There is Cornelius: he has been seeking the Lord, and the Lord is gracious to him, but he must first hear Peter. Over there is a wealthy Ethiopian riding in his chariot, and he is reading the book of the prophet Isaiah, but he cannot understand it until Philip comes. Lydia has a ready heart, but only Paul can lead her to the Lord Jesus.

The instances of souls blessed by human instrumentality are innumerable, but I will conclude by calling attention to one passage upon which I want to briefly dwell. When the prodigal came home, the father did not say to one of his servants, "Go and meet him." No, but we read, *While he was still a long way off, his father saw him and felt compassion for him, and ran and embraced him and kissed him* (Luke 15:20). He did all this himself. The father personally forgave him and restored him; but we read further on that the father said to his servants, *Quickly bring out the best robe and put it on him, and put a ring on his hand and sandals on his feet; and bring the fattened calf, kill it, and let us eat and celebrate* (Luke 15:22-23). The loving father could have done all this himself, but he wanted all the servants in the house to be of one accord with him in the joyful reception of his son.

The great Lord could do everything for a sinner Himself, but He does not do so because He wants all of us to be in fellowship with Him. Come, fellow servants, and bring forth the best robe. I am never happier than when I preach the righteousness of Christ and try to put it upon the sinner. "What!" someone explains. "You cannot put it on!" Yet the parable says, *Bring out the best robe and put it on him.* I not only bring it out and show it, but by the Holy Spirit's help I try to put it on the sinner. I hold it up before him, just as you hold up a friend's coat to help him put it on. You have to guide the poor sinner's hand into the sleeve and lift it up upon his shoulders, or he might never get it on. You are to teach him, comfort him, encourage him, and, in fact, help him to be dressed like one of the family.

Then cannot we also bring out the ring? Certainly the father should have put the ring upon his son's hand, but no, he tells his servants to do that. He says to them, *Put a ring on his hand.* Introduce him into fellowship and make him glad with the communion of saints. We must guide the new convert into the joys of Christian society, letting him know what it is to be married to Christ and joined to His people. We must put honor upon these redeemed ones, and we must adorn those who once were degraded.

Let us not neglect to put shoes on his feet, too! He has a long journey to go. He is to be a pilgrim, and we must help him prepare his feet with *the preparation of the gospel of peace* (Ephesians 6:15). His feet are new in the Lord's ways; we must show him how to run on the Master's errands. As for the fatted calf, it is our duty to feed the redeemed ones. As for the music and the dancing, it is our honor to make the hearts of the repentant ones glad by rejoicing over them.

There is plenty to be done. O my brethren, try and do some of it today. Some people will immediately be looking out for an inquirer, and they will try to put a ring on his hand and shoes on his feet. I wish that more of you did this, but if you cannot do so right here and now, begin as soon as you can. Begin a holy work for the converted who are not yet brought into liberty. There are children of God who do not yet have a shoe on their foot. There are plenty of shoes in the house, but no servant has put them on. When I look around, I see some who do not have the ring on their hand. Oh, that I might have the privilege of putting it on!

I urge you, brethren, by the blood that bought you, by the love that holds you, and by the supreme abundance that supplies your need, go forth and do what your Master graciously allows and commands you to do. Loose Lazarus. Bring forth the best robe and put it on him. Put a ring on his hand and shoes on his feet, and let us all eat and rejoice with our Father. Amen.

# Charles H. Spurgeon – A Brief Biography

Charles Haddon Spurgeon was born on June 19, 1834, in Kelvedon, Essex, England. He was one of seventeen children in his family (nine of whom died in infancy). His father and grandfather were Nonconformist ministers in England. Due to economic difficulties, eighteen-month-old Charles was sent to live with his grandfather, who helped teach Charles the ways of God. Later in life, Charles remembered looking at the pictures in *Pilgrim's Progress* and in *Foxe's Book of Martyrs* as a young boy.

Charles did not have much of a formal education and never went to college. He read much throughout his life though, especially books by Puritan authors.

Even with godly parents and grandparents, young Charles resisted giving in to God. It was not until he was fifteen years old that he was born again. He was on his way to his usual church, but when a heavy snowstorm prevented him from getting there, he turned in at a little Primitive Methodist chapel. Though there were only about fifteen people in attendance, the preacher spoke from Isaiah 45:22: *Look unto me, and be ye saved, all the ends of the earth.* Charles Spurgeon's eyes were opened and the Lord converted his soul.

He began attending a Baptist church and teaching Sunday school. He soon preached his first sermon, and then when he was sixteen years old, he became the pastor of a small Baptist church in Cambridge. The church soon grew to over four hundred people, and Charles Spurgeon, at the age of nineteen, moved on to become the pastor of the New Park Street Church in London. The church grew from a few hundred attenders to a few thousand. They built an addition to the church, but still needed more room to accommodate the congregation. The Metropolitan Tabernacle was built in London in 1861, seating more than 5,000 people. Pastor Spurgeon preached the simple message of the cross, and thereby attracted many people who wanted to hear God's Word preached in the power of the Holy Spirit.

On January 9, 1856, Charles married Susannah Thompson. They had twin boys, Charles and Thomas. Charles and Susannah loved each other deeply, even amidst the difficulties and troubles that they faced in life, including health problems. They helped each other spiritually, and often together read the writings of Jonathan Edwards, Richard Baxter, and other Puritan writers.

Charles Spurgeon was a friend of all Christians, but he stood firmly on the Scriptures, and it didn't please all who heard him. Spurgeon believed in and preached on the sovereignty of God, heaven and hell, repentance, revival, holiness, salvation through Jesus Christ alone, and the infallibility and necessity of the Word of God. He spoke against worldliness and hypocrisy among Christians, and against Roman Catholicism, ritualism, and modernism.

One of the biggest controversies in his life was known as the "Down-Grade Controversy." Charles Spurgeon believed that some pastors of his time were "down-grading" the faith by compromising with the world or the new ideas of the age. He said that some pastors were denying the inspiration of the Bible, salvation by faith alone, and the truth of the Bible in other areas, such as creation. Many pastors who believed what Spurgeon condemned were not happy about this, and Spurgeon eventually resigned from the Baptist Union.

Despite some difficulties, Spurgeon became known as the "Prince of Preachers." He opposed slavery, started a pastors' college, opened an orphanage, led in helping feed and clothe the poor, had a book fund for pastors who could not afford books, and more.

Charles Spurgeon remains one of the most published preachers in history. His sermons were printed each week (even in the newspapers), and then the sermons for the year were re-issued as a book at the end of the year. The first six volumes, from 1855-1860, are known as *The Park Street Pulpit*, while the next fifty-seven volumes, from 1861-1917 (his sermons continued to be published long after his death), are known as *The Metropolitan Tabernacle Pulpit*. He also oversaw a monthly magazine-type publication called *The Sword and the Trowel*, and Spurgeon wrote many books, including *Lectures to My Students, All of Grace, Around the Wicket Gate, Advice for Seekers, John Ploughman's Talks, The Soul Winner, Words of Counsel for Christian Workers, Cheque Book of the Bank of Faith, Morning and Evening*, his autobiography, and more, including some commentaries, such as his twenty-year study on the Psalms – *The Treasury of David*.

Charles Spurgeon often preached ten times a week, preaching to an estimated ten million people during his lifetime. He usually preached from only one page of notes, and often from just an outline. He read about six books each week. During his lifetime, he had read *The Pilgrim's Progress* through more than one hundred times. When he died, his personal library consisted of more than 12,000 books. However, the Bible always remained the most important book to him.

Spurgeon was able to do what he did in the power of God's Holy Spirit because he followed his own advice – he met with God every morning before meeting with others, and he continued in communion with God throughout the day.

Charles Spurgeon suffered from gout, rheumatism, and some depression, among other health problems. He often went to Menton, France, to recuperate and rest. He preached his final sermon at the Metropolitan Tabernacle on June 7, 1891, and died in France on January 31, 1892, at the age of fifty-seven. He was buried in Norwood Cemetery in London.

Charles Haddon Spurgeon lived a life devoted to God. His sermons and writings continue to influence Christians all over the world.

# Other Similar Titles

**Life in Christ (Vol. 1 & 2),**
**by Charles H. Spurgeon**

Men who were led by the hand or groped their way along the wall to reach Jesus were touched by his finger and went home without a guide, rejoicing that Jesus Christ had opened their eyes. Jesus is still able to perform such miracles. And, with the power of the Holy Spirit, his Word will be expounded and we'll watch for the signs to follow, expecting to see them at once. Why shouldn't those who read this be blessed with the light of heaven? This is my heart's inmost desire.

– Charles H. Spurgeon

*Available where books are sold.*

***Words of Warning*,
by Charles H. Spurgeon**

This book, *Words of Warning*, is an analysis of people and the gospel of Christ. Under inspiration of the Holy Spirit, Charles H. Spurgeon sheds light on the many ways people may refuse to come to Christ, but he also shines a brilliant light on how we can be saved. Unsaved or wavering individuals will be convicted, and if they allow it, they will be led to Christ. Sincere Christians will be happy and blessed as they consider the great salvation with which they have been saved.

*Available where books are sold.*

**_Jesus Came to Save Sinners,_ by Charles H. Spurgeon**

This is a heart-level conversation with you, the reader. Every excuse, reason, and roadblock for not coming to Christ is examined and duly dealt with. If you think you may be too bad, or if perhaps you really are bad and you sin either openly or behind closed doors, you will discover that life in Christ is for you too. You can reject the message of salvation by faith, or you can choose to live a life of sin after professing faith in Christ, but you cannot change the truth as it is, either for yourself or for others. As such, it behooves you and your family to embrace truth, claim it for your own, and be genuinely set free for now and eternity. Come and embrace this free gift of God, and live a victorious life for Him.

*Available where books are sold.*

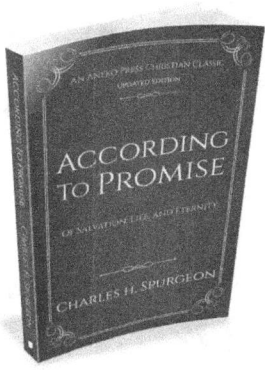

### *According to Promise,*
### by Charles H. Spurgeon

The first part of this book is meant to be a sieve to separate the chaff from the wheat. Use it on your own soul. It may be the most profitable and beneficial work you have ever done. He who looked into his accounts and found that his business was losing money was saved from bankruptcy.

The second part of this book examines God's promises to His children. The promises of God not only exceed all precedent, but they also exceed all imitation. No one has been able to compete with God in the language of liberality. The promises of God are as much above all other promises as the heavens are above the earth.

*Available where books are sold.*

**Words of Counsel, by Charles H. Spurgeon**

Is there any occupation as profitable or rewarding as that of winning souls for Christ? It is a desirable employment, and the threshold for entry into this profession is set at a level any Christian may achieve – you must only love the Lord God with all your heart, soul, and mind; and your fellow man as yourself. This work is for all genuine Christians, of all walks of life. This is for you, fellow Christian.

*Available where books are sold.*

**The Soul Winner, by Charles H. Spurgeon**

As Christians, our main business is to win souls. But, in Spurgeon's own words, "like shoeing-smiths, we need to know a great many things. Just as the smith must know about horses and how to make shoes for them, so we must know about souls and how to win them for Christ." Learn about souls, and how to win them, from one of the most acclaimed soul winners of all time.

*Available where books are sold.*

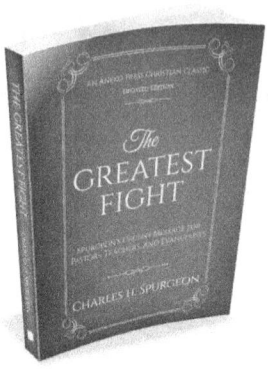

### *The Greatest Fight,*
### by Charles H. Spurgeon

This book examines three things that are of utmost importance in this fight of faith. The first is *our armory*, which is the inspired Word of God. The second is *our army*, the church of the living God, which we must lead under our Lord's command. The third is *our strength*, by which we wear the armor and use the sword.

*Available where books are sold.*

***Come Ye Children,*** **by Charles H. Spurgeon**

Teaching children things of the Lord is an honor and a high calling. Children have boundless energy and may appear distracted, but they are capable of understanding biblical truths even adults have a hard time grasping. Children's minds are easily impressed with new thoughts, whether good or bad, and will remember many of their young lessons for the rest of their life. Adults and churches tend to provide entertainment to occupy the children, but children ought to have our undivided attention. Jesus said, let the little children come to me. They were worthy of His time and devotion, and they are worthy of ours.

*Available where books are sold.*

***Following Christ*, by Charles H. Spurgeon**

You cannot have Christ if you will not serve Him. If you take Christ, you must take Him in all His qualities. You must not simply take Him as a Friend, but you must also take Him as your Master. If you are to become His disciple, you must also become His servant. God-forbid that anyone fights against that truth. It is certainly one of our greatest delights on earth to serve our Lord, and this is to be our joyful vocation even in heaven itself: *His servants shall serve Him: and they shall see His face* (Revelation 22:3-4).

*Available where books are sold.*

***Honest Faith,* by Charles H. Spurgeon**

The paragraphs of this little book are not supposed to be an argument. It was not my aim to convince an opponent but to assist a friend. How I have personally threaded the labyrinth of life thus far may be of helpful interest to some other soul who is in a maze. I hope that these pages will assist some true heart to say "he fought his doubts and gather'd strength." Let no man's heart fail him, for the prevalent skepticisms of today are but "spectres of the mind." Face them, and they fly.

*Available where books are sold.*

www.ingramcontent.com/pod-product-compliance
Lightning Source LLC
Chambersburg PA
CBHW070141080526
44586CB00015B/1794